Haunted Places

Chilling Paranormal and Supernatural Ghost Stories from Around the World

Conrad Bauer

Copyrights

Disclaimer and Terms of Use

ISBN: 978-1544141718

Printed in the United States

MAPLEWOOD
– PUBLISHING –

Contents

Introduction _____ 1

Tower of London, England _____ 3

RMS Queen Mary, California _____ 11

Babenhausen Barracks, Hesse, Germany _____ 23

Ancient Ram Inn, Gloucestershire _____ 31

Lawang Sewu, Indonesia _____ 37

Banff Springs Hotel, Alberta _____ 47

The Myrtles Plantation, St. Francisville, Louisiana _____ 57

Okinawa, Japan _____ 69

Chaonei No. 81 _____ 79

The White House, Washington D.C. _____ 87

Conclusion _____ 93

Further Reading _____ 95

Photo Credits _____ 97

About the author _____ 99

   More Books from Conrad Bauer _____ 100

Introduction

Do you know what lies behind every door? There are certain buildings that can be unsettling, disturbing, and downright terrifying. Even in seemingly normal homes, the strange and mysterious can help to create a sense of unease and ill-feeling. But there are certain buildings that scream strangeness from every surface. A coldness, an eerie atmosphere, or even the half-caught sight of something moving in the corner of your vision. Some homes breathe paranormal activity and can leave you scared before you've even stepped over the threshold.

In this book, we will look at some of the world's most haunted homes, buildings, and places. They are scattered across the world, proving that the unexplained and the terrifying can cross borders and is not restricted to one particular location or culture. We will look at homes, hospitals, boats, and government buildings, all of which contain a history of dark acts. There's nothing to say what might cause a place to become haunted, but there are certain similarities that we can trace from location to location.

Murder, slaughter, torture, and all other forms of gruesome acts serve to leave an imprint. When you walk into these rooms, you can sense the evil deeds that took place. The hairs of on the back of your neck might prickle, the skin on your arms crawl, as you step onto the spot where someone was butchered hundreds of years ago. Often, these events are unexplainable. But in this book, we will attempt to gather the stories together and illustrate the reality of the world's most haunted places.

Tower of London, England

We start with one of the most famous buildings in the world. Anyone who has visited London will likely have seen the castle turrets and spires as they rise up above the River Thames. The Tower of London has dominated the city for centuries, playing a key role in the rule of many monarchs. As a building, its current fame is mostly as a tourism attraction. But its real history is much darker. At various points in time, it has been a military barracks, a prison, a torture chamber, and a place in which enemies of the Kings and Queens of England could be subjected to a great deal of pain before being made to disappear. At times, it has even been home to the collection of strange and wonderful animals that the British collected when they ventured abroad to expand their empire. Over time, a great many people have died within its grounds, and this has created a pervading sense of dread that overcomes those who stay there too long.

If such a high number of people are going to be executed in one place, then it should stand to reason that the violent manner of death would lead to an increase in the negative aura surrounding the building. Having now stood for 900 years, first being erected by William the Conqueror, the Tower has claimed some of the country's worst enemies and permitted the acts of some of its worst rulers. Between visions of Anne Boleyn, Thomas Beckett, and Sir Walter Raleigh, others have reported seeing visions of more common men and women, people whose deaths may have been less memorable but were far more violent. One of the most famous comes from a curious magazine article published in 1860.

The article, like many Victorian publications concerned with the terrifying and the gothic, was published after an intrigued reader but sought clarification of stories he had heard of a haunting that appeared at the Tower of London. In response, the magazine was able to publish a first-hand account from someone who had encountered the ghost itself. At first, the author took great credit to establish his authenticity. Though old, he referred to a number of friends who could attest to his truthful nature. They stated that he rarely exaggerated or indulged his memories. What followed was a strange encounter that was demonstrative of the experiences many people faced when left alone in the Tower after dark.

In 1814, a man named Edmund Swifte was awarded the position of the Keeper of the Crown Jewels. These valuable items are housed to this day in the Tower and have long been considered one of the world's most expensive collections of jewellery. Not only are they laced in finery, but they are coated in the kind of rich history that imbues them with a story and a past that is unmatched by other items. But the past is not one of benevolent rule. By the time the 19th century arrived, the Crown Jewels, symbols of the entire British monarchy, were tainted by countless deaths and stained by the blood of millions. The wars fought on

British soil, in Ireland, in Europe, and in the far-flung corners of the Empire had resulted in a huge number of violent deaths. When he was appointed, Edmund guarded the jewels that represented some of the worst crimes of the British nation, the bloodshed exercised in order to turn the nation into the world's preeminent superpower.

As Keeper of the Crown Jewels, Edmund was trusted with one of the most valuable representations of the British Monarchy. Such was the importance of his job that he and his family were encouraged to take up residence in the tower and to dedicate a large amount of their time to the care and safeguarding of the Jewels. Swifte worked in the position for thirty-eight years. Edmund Swift's most chilling experience in the Tower came three years after he had arrived. Still unsure of the building's secrets at that stage, the night stuck with him forever.

It was a Saturday night. Unlike today, the Tower of London was not a popular tourist destination. At the time, it was still very much a government and military facility. This was back before the crown spent so long washing the blood from the walls and selling tickets to interested sightseers. It was night-time, around the point in the evening known as the Witching Hour. Edmund Swifte was sitting with his wife, his small boy, and his sister-in-law. They occupied what was known as Jewel House, the living quarters that came with his position. Eating a small supper, the group chatted and prepared themselves to get to bed.

The living quarters afforded to Edmund and his family had not always been designated for the Keeper of the Jewels. Instead, the section of the Tower had been recently modernized and made livable for civilians after centuries of being put to a different use. The rooms were once used to keep Anne Boleyn locked up in the days before her execution, while Oliver Cromwell once housed ten bishops in the rooms, locked up until he was able to determine their political use. Incredibly wrapped up in the

5

Tower's long history, the rooms – though now a comfortable living space – lived and breathed the history of the Tower as much as anywhere else. Though more comfortable than many of the rooms in the fortification, the Keeper's quarters were nevertheless a lonely and isolated section when the darkness fell.

The room was not regularly shaped. There were three doors and two windows, which presented a particular difficulty to the builders in a fortress where the walls were up to nine feet thick. The room's chimney projected out from the wall, cut into the room, and was used to hang a large oil painting. On that particular night, the family sat with all of the doors closed. The curtains had been drawn, and being made from particularly heavy and dark materials, were incredibly successful at keeping out any hint of life or light. As such, the only light in the room came from a pair of candles that had been positioned on the table.

The family was sitting around the candles with Edmund at the head of the table, his son to his right, his sister-in-law to his left, and his wife facing opposite. Upstairs, a nurse taking care of the remaining children was putting them to sleep. The family was eating and drinking together, trying to make the most of the night as winter was drawing in. To lighten the mood and in spite of the hour, Edmund offered his wife a glass of wine mixed with a little water. Just as she was about to put the drink to her lips, she burst out with a scream. Raising her hand and pointing to the center of the table, Edmund dropped his head to look where she was pointing.

A cylindrical figure was rising up out of the surface between the two candles. Appearing almost like a shimmering glass tube, it was rising up and up, creeping further into the room. It was almost the thickness of a man's arm and rose up until it was halfway between the ceiling and the table. There seemed to be something inside the material, a denser fluid glimpsed between the ghostly veils of the cylinder. It seemed white and pale, almost like a tumultuous summer cloud that was railing against the outer barriers. It hung there, in the room, the family was stunned into silence, and the materials inside the figure rolling around and around with an increasing restlessness.

Though he could not remember exactly how long the family was stunned into silence watching the apparition, Edmund recalls that roughly two minutes later it began to move. Drifting silently, it positioned itself before the sister-in-law. Next, it moved before the young boy, before moving into place directly in front of Edmund himself. Finally, with an almost purposeful drifting, it began to pass across the table and directly through Edmund's wife. It paused for a moment, just as it was near her right shoulder.

Just as the cylindrical figure nestled on the shoulder of Edmund's wife, she dropped to the floor, clasping both hands to her upper arm and chest, screaming out that, in the name of God, the specter has seized her. Edmund jumped from his chair, kicked it back across the room, and desperately lurched across the room to help his wife.

The apparition was already gone from the room, disappearing through the wooden paneling on the wall behind the screaming woman. Edmund struck the place where the specter had vanished but to no avail. Next, he ran up the stairs as fast as he could, bursting into the room of the nurse, who was putting the other children to bed. From elsewhere in the home, other servants and helpers began to run toward the Keeper of the Jewels, terrified and needing to know what had happened. When the story was revealed to them, there was a hushed silence and many made the sign of the cross over their chest.

But arriving back in the living room where the incident had taken place, Edmund began to talk with his sister-in-law and his son. Seemingly, neither had seen the apparition as it appeared above the table and then fled from the room. Edmund described the event as being somewhere between a marvel and an absurdity. How could the only other two people in the room not have seen what had attacked his wife? He took the problem to the local chaplain and told him of the problem. The chaplain seemed unconvinced, putting forward the idea that it might simply have been a shared deception of the natural senses. But Edmund was certain there was more to it. His wife, still reeling from the attack, knew even more so.

The event plagued upon Edmund's mind over the coming weeks. With little in the way of evidence apart from what he and his wife had seen, there was little that could be done to convince many of the more doubtful members of the community. The Tower was buzzing with the story, and not long after, a story came to Edmund about a group of girls who had been entertaining themselves within the bounds of the castle. Some of the young ladies who occasioned the Tower of London had taken it upon themselves to conduct a number of "phantasmagorical experiments" next to their windows. These summoning incantations had been seemingly ineffectual, and the windows themselves far from the Keeper's quarters. Nevertheless, Edmund made sure to have an extra guard posted to overlook the windows in question.

The story was not over. A few nights later, one of the sentries who had been posted around the home by Edmund reported a strange event. When he had been standing up late at night, overlooking the building housing the Crown Jewels, he had ben astonished to see the large, looming shape of a bear. It was on the other side of a door from the guard, but he still made an effort to attack. Taking the bayonet fastened to the end of his gun, the man rammed it into the wood. The knife was immediately fastened into place and couldn't be moved. The man himself dropped to the ground in a fit and had to be carried into the guards' quarters to recover. After talking to the man, Edmund was satisfied that he had not been drunk and had not fallen asleep. This story was confirmed by a fellow guard, who had been stationed nearby and had seen the man just minutes before. The frightened guard could not recover. Within a few days, the appearance of the ghostly bear had been enough to deliver a "fatal result" and he passed away.

As it appeared in the magazine pages, Edmund Swifte's account is one of the best first-hand stories of ghosts appearing at the Tower of London. A high ranking man and one whose word was implicitly trusted, the stories align with other recollections that have passed down through the ages. While we might struggle to understand the exact nature of his ghastly specter, we do know that the Tower was home to a very large bear during its history, one who was kept on a long chain and allowed to wander down to the banks of the Thames to drink.

In addition to Swifte's story, the members of the public who read through Notes & Queries magazine in the 19th Century also wrote in to share their similar experiences. Though much shorter and from sources not quite as reliable as Swifte, the editor saw fit to publish them anyway.

One of these stories was centered on a small paved yard that had been in place for some years, joining the Jewel House to the Mint, which was reached by passing down a "gloomy and ghostlike" set of stairs to arrive at a doorway. The yard was rendered unusable after the nearby armory burned down but would often be the source for many people to hear strange and odd noises emanating throughout the tower. The replier also reports sightings of a bear-like figure, crossing out into the yard and down the gloomy steps. Just like his fellow guard, the sentry who spotted the apparition soon fell ill and died. In addition to other sightings of the bear, accounts of noises, figures, sudden coldness, and a pervading sense of dread were reported among those who worked full time at the Tower and especially by those who worked at night.

These first-hand accounts of hauntings at the Tower of London do nothing to relate the building's extremely violent past. Take, for example, the story of the Countess of Salisbury. Convicted of standing up to Henry VIII, she was held in the Tower for two and a half years before being told one morning that she would be executed. Set for beheading that morning, she refused to lay her head across the chopping block. The guards held her in place while an inexperienced executioner prepared his axe. When he delivered what was intended to be the killer blow, the axe only served to cut the Countess along the shoulder. He needed ten more blows before the bloody affair was finally over and the woman's head fell from her neck. Some people have even said that the Countess leapt up after the first blow and was chased around by the executioner, who swung the axe as he chased her. When inspecting her cell, the jailors found that she had carved a poem into the wall demanding forgiveness from God and protesting her innocence. Her ghost is said to wander the halls of the Tower, sometimes with a head, sometimes without.

The Tower of London might be one of the most haunted buildings in the world, and it might well have one of the bloodiest histories. But these days, it is little more than a tourist destination. As we read through this guide, we will begin to look at buildings that are far more eerie, mysterious, and much less welcoming to sightseers.

RMS Queen Mary, California

A haunted building is not necessarily bricks and mortar. While the majority of locations we will look at during this exploration will constitute conventional buildings, our next entry is something entirely different but no less eerie. The RMS Queen Mary is an ocean liner, built in the 1930s to transport people over the world's vast expanses of water. These huge ships are often like condensed, self-contained cities. They have residential areas, markets, doctors, and – below deck – a furnace and factory conditions needed to heave nearly 4,000 people and over 80,000 tons of iron and steel across the water's surface. Just as with any city or town, everyday people live their lives on board. When at sea, they are often hundreds of miles from land and civilization as we might know it. This means that those on board have to cope with births, illnesses, and – eventually – deaths. These deaths can be violent, sudden, and premature. Often, they can leave a ghostly imprint on the vessel itself.

The Queen Mary is now retired. It no longer hauls people across the world in various levels of luxury. Instead, it has been repurposed as a stationary, floating hotel. Now docked in California, those interested in the 1930s' most ostentatious modes of travel can book in to a few nights and discover the privileges of the ocean-going experience without ever once leaving the dock. But the boat remembers. Despite its seemingly innocent current iteration, the Queen Mary has a reputation for the paranormal. It is known as one of the most haunted locations in America. Even if it is no longer at sea, that has not stopped the pervading sense of dread that can often creep over those who choose to stay on board.

The Queen Mary spent thirty-one years at sea. During that time, she endured some of the worst storms and most severe weather conjured up by Mother Nature. She witnessed many deaths. Some of these were natural, the passing away of the sometimes elderly patients as they shuffled off their mortal coils. Others were less expected. One of the worst losses of life came when the Queen Mary crashed into a military vessel, the HMS Curacoa. During World War II, many such ships were conscripted by the governments around the world and used for military purposes. The Queen Mary's sheer size meant that she was capable of transporting as many as 15,000 men across the ocean, from one theatre of war to another. In order to limit the danger to ships posed by German U-Boats, a common tactic was to travel with a number of escort ships in a convoy. Like herds of zebra worried about the attack of the lions, the sheer number of vessels in these groups acted to protect individual ships.

In October of 1942, the Queen Mary was travelling with the HMS Curacoa. The Queen Mary, carrying thousands of American troops to the western front, was under strict instructions that it should stop under no circumstances. The HMS Curacoa was transporting both Italian and German prisoners of war, and just

12

off the coast of Ireland, the two boats collided. The Queen Mary, the much bigger ship, simply ploughed through the Curacoa and left it sinking in her wake. Not stopping, as per orders, she made port with a broken stem. However, back at sea, the loss of life was huge. There are thought to have been as many as 239 people who plunged into the freezing waters that day and perished as a result.

But the deaths surrounding the Queen Mary were not limited to the war. For the last thirty years, people have attempted to delve deeper in the mysteries of the ship. What makes this difficult is that deaths may well have been covered up during the course of the ship's lifetime, as to not cause the other passengers to panic during the longer passages of voyages. Investigations, therefore, can often come up against the dead end of an incomplete report or deliberate misinformation.

One of the most persistent legends and rumors, however, revolves around one specific cabin on board the ship. B340 has become known as one of the epicenters of paranormal activity on board. It is said that the spirit of a murder victim lingers in the cabin, one of 49 people (both crew and passengers) who are known to have passed away while on the Queen Mary. In addition to this, the ship's nursery is allegedly the location in which numerous people have reported hearing strange noises and calls, particularly those that sound like children playing. When moving in to inspect more closely, the nursery is just as abandoned as it has been for the last half a century. Members of the Curacoa have been witnessed haunting the Queen Mary, searching for the ship's captain who gave the order not to stop and search for survivors. While the engine room is supposedly the home to a crew member who perished at the hands of the ship's gigantic internal mechanisms, an unnamed lady dressed in white has been glimpsed in the corridors of the ship, though no one has as of yet managed to discern who she is nor how she was killed. Some the more gruesome stories are: a little girl who fell to her death down a stairwell; one of the ship's officers who accidently died after drinking poison; and one young boy who found himself caught in one of the ship's heavy watertight doors.

Many of the ghostly apparitions aboard the ship have involved drowning victims. On an ocean-going vessel that frequently carried thousands of passengers over the turbulent Atlantic, it should come as no surprise that falling overboard was almost an instant death sentence and a cause to stay vigilant whenever one was near the deck. However, researchers have noted that of the near fifty deaths recorded in the ship's logs, none of them have been attributed to drowning. Three quarters of these reported deaths occurred among members of the crew, while the remaining quarter were all passengers. Records for possible deaths occurring during the Queen Mary's time spent being used by the military were not recorded, or if they were, they have not been released by the United States military. In short, we have little clue as to the exact number of people who died aboard the vessel. Attempts to uncover the boat's paranormal past have often come up against a lack of information, which may be either accidental or deliberate. What we do know is that the Queen Mary has seen more death during her tenure than older buildings witness across many centuries.

Stories about ghosts on the Queen Mary can be traced back to her days in use as an ocean liner. When she made port for the final time, she checked into a dry dock and the workmen began to look her over for repairs and issues. As they worked on the ship, figures appeared fleetingly at the edge of vision, or conversations floated down from nowhere. When they moved to investigate, they would return to find that their tools had been moved, only to find them later in strange corners of the ship. According to some, these restless spirits were those of the dead who had grown used to sailing the seas and were voicing their displeasure at having to be set in a single dock. Others have argued that the damage wrought inside the ship when converting it from an ocean liner to a hotel angered those who had grown used to the surroundings. Estimates of the exact number of spirits aboard the vessel and their motivations have fluctuated greatly, but there has been a consensus reached on a few, figures who have been repeatedly seen across the decades.

One of the most famous of all the apparitions aboard the Queen Mary is a young girl known as Jacqueline Torin, or Jackie for short. When noted paranormal investigator Peter James arrived on the boat in 1991 to look into the various claims of hauntings, one of the first encounters he had was with a girl who was as young as five or six. She was found, at first, inside the Royal Theatre. The room was quiet when they entered, but on detecting a strange presence in the room, James reached out and asked aloud whether there was another presence anywhere nearby. He received an answer. A girl's voice spoke out amid the empty theatre, telling him to meet in the "other pool."

For James, this was a confusing message. By the time he arrived on the Queen Mary, the retrofitting of the insides was complete. What was now the Royal Theatre had once been the swimming pool designated for use by the second class passengers. The "other pool" was a reference to the first class pool, located elsewhere. With little knowledge of the original layout of the ship, James had to turn back to his notes in order to track down the original layout of the vessel and make his way to the first class pool. What he didn't know was that the "other pool" was a notorious hotbed of paranormal activity and one of the key places aboard the ship where people had reported strange encounters. Nevertheless, he ventured forth to find Jackie and the pool she had described. When he arrived, he was able to share a private conversation with the girl, delivered in a hoarse whisper, lasting for all of ten minutes before the girl went away. This would be the first, tangible encounter with one of the spirits who would become a famed resident of the Queen Mary.

Peter James's encounter with Jackie may have been the first, but more and more information has come to light as further people claimed to have met the young girl while aboard the Queen Mary. Those who say they have talked to her tell tales of a playful girl, one who spends her time having fun with anyone she encounters by playing games such as hide and seek. Making noises, running and hiding again, or moving people's possessions while appearing on the balcony on the upper part of the ship seem to be her favored activities. Getting a glimpse of the youngster remains difficult, however, and few report more than fleeting glimpses of a ghostly figure who has quickly vanished. Often, this can be all part of a game.

Though it might sound as though Jackie is one of the more spirited, positive apparitions, there is a chilling side to her story. Those who have not gone looking for her, but rather have wandered into the pool by mistake, have sometimes returned with tales of a child's voice calling out for her mother. Many have speculated that the girl was last aboard the ship during the war years, and that her mother was one of the many "war brides" who existed during the time. These were women who married men from another country, such as Australian women who met American soldiers, during the war and tried to settle down. Though their husbands were displaced, they found themselves having to travel to a foreign culture to await news of their new husbands' possible death. Jackie, perhaps, was one of the daughters of these women, who died during the crossing to America and was forgotten amid the upheaval of the war years. During her voyage, she drowned in the second class pool, possibly after her mother expected to find her in the first class venue. Caught between the two pools, she drowned without anyone to keep an eye on her. Now, she roams the areas between the two pools searching for the mother she lost, reaching out to try and rediscover what traces of family she left aboard the Queen Mary.

Another encounter with Jackie was recorded by Frank Beruecos, who retold the story many times over the years. A fellow paranormal investigator, he looked over the work done by Peter James and decided that the Queen Mary was worth a visit of his own. Among the vast potential for paranormal happenings on the ship, the story about the little girl lost in the swimming pool particularly stuck with him. But the possibility of ghosts was not the only thing that drew him to the ship. To those who have never visited, it can be hard to picture the actual beauty of one of the most luxurious ocean liners that ever existed. Back in the 1930s, when it was built, the chance to fly over the Atlantic Ocean in first class seats was not available. Instead, the journey would take far longer. As people had money to pay, the ship builders realized that the insides of their vessels would need to be more like the traditional stately homes than most boats. The Queen Mary is a fine example of this. When compared to her modern replacement, the difference in ostentatious, Art Deco garnishing is obvious. For those who paid top dollar, the Queen Mary was an incredible place to spend a fortnight when crossing the ocean. But such luxury provided a tragic backdrop to the various tales of death. Frank wanted to learn more about the unique and beautiful location of Queen Mary, its history, and Jackie in particular.

The first class pool room was a well-known hub of ghostly activity aboard the ship. It seemed to attract the paranormal with a spectral magnetism that is hardtop quantify. For those who go looking explicitly for ghosts, however, they can often be disappointed. Many of the best and most interesting stories occur to those who happen across the room by mistake or who find themselves in the pool after hours. Frank, however, knew that this was one of the most important places he would need to visit when aboard the Queen Mary. One of the attributes of the first class pool room that can so often trap the unsuspecting is the labyrinth of the corridors one must take in order to reach the right place. These twisting, dark hallways can often look alike and can make it very hard to tell whether you are heading in the right direction or simply walking around in circles. Placed right at the heart of the ship, well away from the stern, the bow, or even the iron sides of the vessel, there is a strange quiet to the pool and its surroundings that seems almost impossible elsewhere, especially when the Atlantic is hammering against the outer walls.

But Frank's initial investigators turned up nothing. On his first visit, searching for Jackie or any of her friends, he was disappointed to find himself simply sitting alone in the pool room, surrounded by the eerie quiet of the now-docked ship. Elsewhere in the building these days, a bustling hotel trade is conducted and people even go on tours of the Queen Mary. But you would never be able to tell that in the pool room. As well as the quiet, the low lighting only serves to heighten the senses. People search around for any slight changes and differences that might point toward something out of the ordinary. On his first visit, Frank was left alone for hours in the quiet room. No one came forward.

And this was the same on his second visit and his third. For Frank, it seemed, the secrets of the first class pool room were not forthcoming. But that didn't deter him. There is something about the calmness of the room that is alluring, which can sedate and seduce those who are particularly in tune with the paranormal forces. Frank knew that there was something not normal about the room, but he had thus far failed to encourage any spirits to come forward. That was…until he met Jackie.

One night, Frank was sat in his same spot. For the paranormal investigator, the possibility of spending time to witness absolutely nothing was a very real occupational hazard. The chance that he might be sitting all alone in a cold, unfriendly, and uninviting place for hours on end with little to show for it must have been the end result in the vast majority of cases. But every now and again, there was something that could restore the faith. At least in the first class pool room, the environment was relatively comfortable. On the night in question, Frank had teamed up with a fellow professional in order to better his chances of finding answers. One of the most frequent methods of encouraging paranormal activity, particularly among those spirits who you know have interacted with people positively in the past, is to ask questions. That night, Frank and his partner were standing in the pool room, asking questions to Jackie in the hope that she (or anyone else) might answer.

When calling out to the room at large, one of the most direct questions Frank attempted asked whether Jackie would feel comfortable appearing before them. He asked her to appear and was met with nothing. But then, there began to emerge a strange sound. At first, it sounded like nothing, but it grew louder and louder. Soon, it was discernibly the noise of a very young girl, saying over and over, "No, no, no!" This was something. It might have been a negative response, but in the huge number of hours that Frank had spent in the pool room, this was the first response he had actually encountered.

However, Jackie was refusing to appear before the men. Instead, Frank tried to take a different route. This time, he asked Jackie whether she was able to lower the temperature of the entire room. For paranormal investigators, questions such as these – and in particular, the spirits' responses – can be used to discern what exactly they are dealing with. On this occasion, however, the little girl's voice continued. "No, no, no!" It was negative again. For a man who had spent so many fruitless nights alone in the room, even this was progress. Looking questioningly at his partner, Frank managed to confirm that both instances of the responding voice had been caught on tape.

The room stayed the same temperature, and Jackie refused to appear. Frank persisted with his questions but found that other answers were less forthcoming. As he switched to playing with the various monitoring devices they had set up, a strange calmness fell over the room. The low lighting, such a recognizable feature of the first class pool, began to subtly alter. The little lights that were hung around the wall began to dance, flickering on an off gently. It was enough to give the impression of a crackling fire or a candle, rather than the sustained electric light that is common place in the modern age. Rather than electric, it almost felt alive.

By this time, the two men had been in the room for an hour. The questions they had started with had received a response, but Jackie had soon vanished into the gloom. Now, as Frank resumed his questioning, the lights seemed as though they were moving in response to the words. Rather than just one lamp turning on and off, there seemed to be an order and a partner to the movements, almost as though Jackie was trying to respond through another means. But without the means to translate the flickering into words, they were forced to simply document the phenomena. Unable to respond to the specter's messages, however, it seems that Jackie eventually grew weary of playing with the two men and moved on to other areas of the ship. For the rest of the night, the room stayed quiet, and the lights remained strong and constant. After trying to find the ghost of Jacqueline Torin for so long, Frank finally had his encounter.

Events such as these are indicative of the fame that has built up around many of the paranormal apparitions aboard the Queen Mary. As well as Jackie, figures such as the Lady in White and Susan provide similar stories. Indeed, Frank himself tells a tale about one visit to the first class pool room during which he actually witnessed an incredibly strange event. On a night much like the one we have already described, he recalls seeing a shifting black mass rising into the room, visible only really in the corners of his vision. It was almost like a physical shadow, one which moved through the room with amazing speed. The shape has appeared before him a number of times, rising up quickly, and then vanishing up and over the mezzanine area that overlooks the pool. Unlike the voice of Jackie, this particular phenomena has yet to be explained.

The interest that surrounded the ghostly activity aboard the Queen Mary is sure to continue. As investigations search deeper and deeper into the history of the ships, and perhaps as key military records are declassified, we might be able to build up an exact picture of what exactly is haunting one of history's greatest ocean liners.

Babenhausen Barracks, Hesse, Germany

Paranormal mysteries can exist in places for centuries. Over time, people will notice the eerie nature of certain parts of the land and will begin to warn one another of the perilous territory. In places where people have lived for centuries, these locations can go through several incarnations, each bearing the same scars and history, just built up into a different package. Nowhere is this more obvious than in Europe, where the long and twisted history of places such as France, Germany, and Italy has thrown together horrific events with the collected cultural consciousness that can remember and pass down the legends and explanations regarding any ghostly activity in the area.

Even after the turmoil and destruction of two world wars fought across the continent, some of the most haunted places in the world continue to attract interest from those with a specific interest in the macabre and the paranormal. One such place is the Babenhausen Barracks, found in Hesse in Germany. Just south of the center of the country, we can trace some of the more modern tales of fear back to the 19th century and before. Since then, the relatively modern surroundings have not stopped the ancient mysteries creeping into the location and spreading fear and discontent about those who pass through and visit the area. The Babenhausen Barracks have built up a reputation as one of the strangest and most terrifying places in all of Europe, a reputation that has persisted as the various buildings on the site have been bulldozed and rebuilt. This is an enduring legend.

Anyone who travels to Babenhausen will immediately be struck by the flatness of the land. It is located in a stretch of central Germany that has little in the way of high mountains. To the north, the Odenwald rises up out of the ground, while the River Gersprenz has long ago eroded the majority of the local landscape. What emerges is an incredibly flat land, one where a person might be able to look out along the cold plains on a wintry day and see for miles. The local birds, kingfishers and white storks, bustle around the banks of the river, breaking the silence and the calm of an otherwise empty part of the country. Scattered across Babenhausen are the occasional pine forests. Rather than one continuous belt of evergreen trees, there are rather small clusters that crop up occasionally. The trees almost huddle together for warmth and break apart the isolated landscape like small islands on a calm sea. Though they might seem strange, they offer the chance for wildlife and people to hide in a place where most things exist directly in plain sight. Even the ground is slightly different, with the local soil being notorious for its strange white appearance. While this makes it perfect for the growing of asparagus, it can lend a surreal appearance to the earth to anyone who is walking across the countryside.

The history of Babenhausen as a community often revolves around the local castle. Built in the 12th century, the small, low-topped building offers little for those who have been seduced by the aesthetics of the spiraling Bavarian fortresses. Instead, its small, squat nature allies itself well to the flat ruggedness of the landscape. The local lords of Babenhausen have come and gone over the years, having little impact on the history of the area. A thirty-year war in the 18th century was needed to settle one of the fiercest inheritance disputes, but the fighting is often merely a footnote in the history of a country that has seen everything from Roman conquest to the last German retreat of World War II.

World War II actually wrought a great deal of damage to the town. After suffering from the wrath of the various armies in the closing days of the war, it was chosen as one of the key locations for one of the DP (displaced persons) camps set up following Germany's defeat. After the Final Solution had been enacted by Adolf Hitler's Third Reich, the Holocaust had switched up into high gear. The use of concentration camps had allowed for the mass slaughter of those peoples considered unsuitable under the Nazi regime. As the Allied forces finally defeated the Wehrmacht, the liberation of these camps was an essential part of the final days of the war. But afterwards, they were left with masses of people who had been upheaved by the Nazis genocidal plans. Babenhausen was one of the places chosen to house one of the DP sites, which provided a place for these people to stay after they had been liberated from imprisonment in the death camps. These people had been witness to some of the most terrible atrocities wrought by mankind. As they waited to go home, they were left to mull over their experiences in Babenhausen, its bleak surroundings feeding into and feeding off of the negative emotions that they emanated.

Many years after the DP camp was no longer needed, the German military turned the facility into a base. Today, that base still stands, but it is now used as a war museum. The barracks at the location, however, are not just a simple training facility. While the public was denied access to the location for the majority of the time, this has not stopped the emergence of a number of ghost stories from the base. After a strange history, Babenhausen barracks now has a reputation of being one of the most haunted sites in all of Germany. But if we are going to trace some of the stranger paranormal moments that have occurred in the area, then we must start with events in the 19th Century.

It is important to note a strange architectural addition to the Babenhausen castle that might give some insight into the paranormal history of the area. The castle features what is known as a "witch tower." There, parts of the castles were built in a more superstitious time, when the accusation and negative implications of witchcraft carried far more weight. Specific to Germany, these witch towers were tall, circular turrets built into the walls of the castle. They often featured a canonical spire, tapering off to a point, a roof that often had a hole built into it. When a person was accused of witchcraft, they would be held in the tower for as long as it took to investigate matters. Should they be found guilty, then the tower would become the scene of their execution. These witch towers were built and used to burn magic users or those accused.

In Babenhausen, much like the rest of Germany at the time, we do not have exact numbers for the numbers of people who were burned or otherwise executed inside these architectural oddities. Later, they became more general-use prisons, but the town of Babenhausen is remembered as the site of one particularly vicious execution. During the 19th century, long after the majority of witchcraft accusations had died down, it seems as though an unnamed woman was discovered in the town and thought to be using magic for nefarious purposes. She was imprisoned in the tower before eventually being found guilty. As she burned, she swore a terrible vengeance on the townspeople who were killing her. To this day, we don't know whether the accusations had any merit or whether an innocent woman was burned to death. What we do know, however, is that the people in the town soon began to experience very odd behavior, incidents, and occurrences, all of which they attributed to the dead woman. Noises in the bushes, animals falling sick, children contracting diseases. The list of negative occurrences grew and grew until the townsfolk were certain that the woman's spirit was lingering around the village with malicious intent. To this day, the ghost of the dead woman is listed as one of the chief causes of paranormal activity and one of the sources of the negative energy that pervades through the barracks and the castle.

But the talk of strange, ghostly activity in the area has carried on. As well as the ghost of the woman burned as a witch, we also have stories from those who were stationed on the base following its conversion from a DP camp. At the time, the German military was still coming to terms with the sheer horror of what had been done during the war years. The soldiers positioned on the base not only had to deal with the stories of those who had been burned as witches (and their continued haunting), but they also moved into the facility after the poor people who had suffered at the Nazi hands had been returned to whatever homes they had left. If paranormal activity can be attributed to the negative emotional energy that accumulates in a place, then the barracks in Babenhausen must surely pull ahead of almost every other place in the world in terms of their own frightful nature.

So the stories continued. Soldiers positioned around the base would often tell tales from the deepest, darkest nights when they were met by what were seemingly colleagues walking through the dark hallways. They might greet one another or share a quick word before departing, and it was only then that the soldier would notice the figure was wearing a uniform out of date by almost twenty years. The prevalence of the WW II soldiers seen on base increased over the years. They would be in hallways and in the roads. Sometimes they might be seen walking forgotten guard routes or searching for dismantled watch towers. They were never glimpsed for very long and often vanished into the night just as quickly as they had been noticed. They were almost like memories of men haunted by their own actions, the guilt-ridden specters of those German troops who had been complicit in the crimes of World War II.

Similarly, the old orders would often make themselves apparent. When answering phones on the base, a common complaint was that the speech appearing on the other end was almost unintelligible. This would usually mean that the person trying to use the phone would simply hang up. But when an investigation into the phenomena was conducted by the high command, it was found that the words were not spoken in English nor German and seemed to be words read backwards. When deciphered or translated, the conversations on the other end of the phone might have been long lists of orders than had been passed to the men previously stationed on the base, the orders that had most particularly troubled the men when they had carried them out. It's common for those stationed in the barracks to hear footsteps with no source, for light switches to be flicked on and off of their own accord, and for voices to emerge whispering from the lower basements.

There was even a selection of stories that emerged in the 1980s that attributed violent acts directly to the ghost of the burned witch. After a series of soldiers were found dead on the site, it forced the authorities to launch a probe into what actually happened. Though the results were never made public, there were rumors and legends of their findings. It was said that the woman's ghost would appear to these men, seducing them, and finally encouraging them to kill themselves in a series of gruesome fashions. Still seeking revenge, the spirit of the woman was blamed for the mysterious deaths. Though we might find haunted houses more in line with the traditional idea of the paranormal, the enduring negative energy and complicated aura of death and evil that surrounds the barracks in Babenhausen give them a distinct edge and ensure that they are a more than worthy entry in this series.

Ancient Ram Inn, Gloucestershire

Sometimes, the paranormal activity in a building can become very famous. In the previous entries in this book, the ghost stories have taken a back seat to the tourism and hotel opportunities offered up by the buildings. The mysteries of the dead play a second fiddle in these instances, an interesting side note to those of a certain persuasion. But when it comes to the Ancient Ram Inn in Gloucestershire, England, the reputation as one of the country's most haunted houses is an essential part of what makes the location so famous. Because of this, it can be difficult to separate the facts from the fiction, the real hints of the paranormal from those that are cooked up by frightful visitors or those who would benefit from the Inn being better known.

Despite this, however, the Ancient Ram Inn does have a long and sordid history. To look at, it certainly seems as though it is a relic of another time. Built in 1145, it is now nearly 900 years old. As is to be expected of any building that has been standing for close to nine centuries, it has certainly seen its fair share of life and death. Those who look upon the building from a distance will notice how it sits snugly into the landscape. The whitewashed walls and the ancient roof have grown heavy with vegetation and ivy, as the countryside has been slowly reclaiming the building. The dark windows seem almost sunken in the greying walls, while the old wood in the frames sags and heaves, likely rotten on the inside. So old is the building, so set in its ways, that it seems incredibly detached from the modern way of life. It is a relic, a proven link to the past. When examining the outside walls, one could be standing before a home built at any time in the last three hundred years. The only modern affectations – guttering and electric lights – are easily overlooked when faced with the daunting façade as it looms above you. If one had to picture an ancient haunted home, then the hotel would fit the bill almost too well.

Once you venture inside, these fears are almost immediately confirmed. The labyrinth building owes little to modern architectural practices and is instantly unfamiliar to anyone who has no experience with navigating a home designed to fit the purpose of life in the 12th Century. The staircase is a fine example of the claustrophobic, tight atmosphere that the Ancient Ram imposes on its guests. The steps themselves are short, close to half a foot across. They are packed tightly together, meaning a steep, treacherous journey up or down the flight, especially in the dark. The handrail is a recent addition, a concession to the difficult nature of the stairs, while the adorations and decoration add to the age. Walking up the stairs, one comes face to face with dusty picture frames and empty bottles on either side, chipped wood that is crying out for a new coat, and a tattered carpet on each step that tries (and fails) to add a sense of warmth to the journey.

The most famous room in the establishment is called the Bishop's room. Said to be the most haunted of all the parts of the building, it sits on the first floor and has caused a great deal of consternation to those who have stayed there. Even before the Inn's reputation was well known, guests who stayed in the Bishop's room would often wake up screaming in the middle of the night and flee in terror. It was stories such as this that helped the Ancient Ram garner its legend as one of the most haunted places, something that now surely plays on the minds of those who choose to spend a night in the Bishop's room. Hearing so much as a creak or a scratch, those who are aware of the legends will likely already have little else on their minds when faced with a night in the haunted room. This adds to the self-perpetuating sense of terror in the establishment, feeding into its own reputation even on those occasions when no paranormal activity is actually detected.

But how has the building come to be so haunted? Legends about the Ancient Ram vary, though more stories have come to light thanks to recent investigations. It is said that there are as many as 20 different ghosts haunting the Inn, though only a few of them have been sighted on a regular basis. The proclivity of the spirits and their attraction toward the property seems to have stemmed from the site itself. Historians have looked into the past, as well as excavation work done in the cellar of the Inn, and all of the facts seem to indicate that the site was once used as a place for pagan rituals. Before the arrival of Christianity in Britain, the druids and their pagan religion was practiced by the Celts and ancient Britons. The lot in Gloucestershire was supposedly used to bury people and animals. It is likely that sacrifices were conducted nearby, the blood spilling into the soil and leaving quite the impression. When Christianity came to Britain, the practice of paganism was eradicated. When the last traces finally disappeared, previous sites of importance such as the Ancient Ram were allegedly used for devil worship and child sacrifice. Whether this is true or simply Christian propaganda, we don't know. What we do know is that the links to such practices have connected the Inn to paganism for many, many centuries.

Added to this, recent excavations by the owners of the Ancient Ram have helped fuel the fire regarding the bloodshed on the site. John Humphries, one of the owners of the Inn was fascinated by the building's sordid past. Venturing down into the cellar, he began the process of excavating the earth under the floor. When he dug down through the concrete floor and into the dirt beneath, he brought out a number of children's bones and ceremonial daggers. These findings have proved contentious, with researchers debating whether they were simply castoffs from assorted sacrifices or whether they were purposefully buried at the site as part of a burial ceremony.

These days, the Inn is owned by John Humphries daughter, Caroline. A firm believer in the Ancient Ram's paranormal past, she welcomes any doubters to spend time in the building to see whether their cynicism can endure the mysterious goings-on that pervade the Inn. She is one of the best people to talk to when in need of more information about the hauntings in the Inn, as she has not only see many of the specters herself, but she had seen the effects they can have on her visitors. There have been tales of furniture being shifted across the room in the dead of night, of a small girl who wanders wistfully along hallways dressed in ancient rags, and even stories about a horseman who charges furiously along the path right up to the front door. These ghosts have, at one time or another, been so powerful as to force guests to desperately look around for a way out. The way the grounds are laid out, there are large, soft tufts of grass between many of the windows, and the things going bump in the night have forced a number of guests to leap from their windows out into the night, rather than stay another second inside the haunted Inn.

But the legends of the ghosts themselves have endured for years. Just as with the haunting at the Babenhausen barracks, many can trace some of the more concerning stories back to an execution that happened in the area. In the 16th Century, it was common practice for those accused of witchcraft to be executed. In this part of Gloucestershire, the site of the Ancient Ram Inn was chosen as the place at which the authorities could burn a woman at the stake after she had been found guilty of nefarious magical practices. As the government and the Church began to exert more and more influence on these kinds of proceedings, the woman's execution was by no means an isolated event. But taking place as it did on an ancient pagan site of importance may have permitted that extra paranormal power that causes spirits to linger and remain in a place. If she were vengeful and displeased, then it is easy to see why she might have taken up residence in one of the rooms and begun to haunt those who came to visit her.

Caroline Humphries can recall times as a child when she was too scared to sleep inside the family house. There was a caravan parked outside, a suitable distance from the home, and the terrified child would prefer to spend her nights out in the mobile home rather than inside the walls of the Ancient Ram Inn. She is not alone. The legend of the Inn has grown enough to welcome those interested in the paranormal. Many people want to stay the night in the Inn, hoping to get a glimpse of the paranormal. While some leave disappointed, others leave running and screaming from the property. With such a mixed experience being shared by those who enter the house, it can be almost impossible to say exactly what it is that lies inside the walls of the Inn, what lies beneath the floor, or what ancient spirits are immortalized in the foundations, bricks, and mortar. If you would like to discover just what amounts to the Ancient Ram's terrifying aura, then you too can spend the night inside its withered walls. With so many stories of the paranormal, this may well be the best way in which to learn more about those locations that blur the line between what we know and the world beyond.

Lawang Sewu, Indonesia

Not every haunted house wants to be a destination for those who are curious about the paranormal. Some locations, such as Lawang Sewu in Indonesia, bear scars brutal enough and recent enough in the physical world to not need any added mysterious quality to their reputation. Built as recently as 1904, the property is one of the newest entries in this book. But at the same time, it is seen as a representation of some of the most violent ideologies of the last few centuries. Constructed by the colonial powers that owned Indonesia at the time, it embodies many of the brutal acts carried out by the regime. For some, however, there is not only the physical past to worry about when discussing Lawang Sewu, but the sensation that these horrific acts left behind a spiritual scar that is yet to heal. Not only a historical manifestation of the country's colonial past, there are also tales that the building has become a focal point for the attraction of ghostly spirits.

These days, Lawang Sewu overlooks one of the city's busiest traffic intersections. Standing opposite the building is a monument, the Tugu Muda, a tribute to those who fought and died in the Indonesian war for independence. Added to this, the nearby military history museum can tell those visiting the city of the important role it played in chasing out the various imperial rulers in the middle of the 20th Century. To the locals, the building is not only famous, but notorious. Everyone knows about it, and introducing it into a conversation will be sure to provoke an energetic response. It is, quite simply, one of the most famous buildings in the country.

But this kind of fame is not quite so simple. The building has played a key role in the various historical narratives that are intertwined with the country's history, but it is the reputation as a home for the paranormal that often dominates the conversation. The architectural achievements of Lawang Sewu, imported from the Dutch colonial masters, are themselves a throwback to the imperial past, but the stories of the revolutionary battles fought on the grounds, the invasion by the Japanese, the executions and torture committed in the buildings, and the tales of the ghosts of those who died meant that picking apart the true history of the mysterious location can be incredibly difficult. If you are at all interested in the gruesome, the vicious, and the macabre, then the history of Lawang Sewu may be of huge interest.

For the local government, this is a problem. The building is a landmark and a recognizable face of the city that is known to all. However, it carries the reputation of an evil and haunted house. As such, the authorities are attempting to cover up and rewrite the history of headless ghouls that wander the corridors, expunging them in favor of creating a thriving tourist destination. This is impossible when many people view the property to be haunted and possessed. But as hard as they try to cover up the truth about the building, people remain acutely aware of the strange tales that have passed out of the walls.

In order to dissect the meaning of Lawang Sewu, it makes sense to start with the name. Etymologically speaking, the words "Lawang Sewu" translate into English as "a thousand doors." This is no doubt a reference to the twisted, complex layout envisioned by the architects. Travel down any one corridor, and you might find yourself surrounded by doors, windows, stairwells, cellar doors, and even secret tunnels. Wherever you look, there is a portal to another part of the building. The building was designed by Cosman Citroen, working on behalf of the Dutch colonialists who were ruling in Indonesia at the time. Created in a contemporary style, it sought to marry the advances of Dutch Rationalism with a more local style, as well as the advancing technologies and innovations that were available in the age. As such, the building was to be seen as a doorway itself. It opens the portal between the Netherlands and Indonesia, between the modern and the old, between east and west. As well as the physical doors that so obviously lend themselves to the name, these bridges between cultures are surely metaphorical inclusions that raise the number of doors out of the physical and into the metaphysical.

The area surrounding Lawang Sewu is home to many examples of similar architectural designs, though none have managed to dominate the public consciousness quite in the same way. Working throughout the latter half of the 19th Century and the early 20th Century, the Dutch transformed much of this part of the city and left it aesthetically reminiscent of their rule. Ground was broken on the site of the Lawang Sewu in 1904, though it took another three years to complete the main section, commonly known as the "A building." After that, it would be another twelve years before the rest of the complex was complete, during which time the builders added two huge, identical towers to the A building that so often catch the eye. These towers were both originally designed for the purpose of storing water. Each one can hold nearly 1,800 United States gallons.

These two towers give an indication as to the original purpose of the building. Built by the Dutch East Indies Railway Company, it was designed to be the first home of the country's railroad network. The Dutch East Indies Company built up a reputation throughout the region, where they were known for their savage rule. Much like the traditional steam engine stations, the water towers that flank the A building give Lawang Sewu a distinctive appearance and immediately mark it out as something familiar and strange at the same time. It is a grand western railway station built in a country that did not yet possess the railway network warranting such an expenditure. But it was heralded as a sign of things to come for the Dutch rulers in the country. They expanded the complex to include a "B building," with a giant tunnel system linking the various parts of the site.

While it might once have been an impressive sight, the Lawang Sewu of the modern era – and much of the surrounding colonial architecture – has fallen into disrepair. There is a hint of neglect and a stench of decay among these buildings. To combat this, there have been attempts to paint over the rot in the former railway house, the local government believing that their iconic building has something to offer beyond the traditional ghost stories.

The original purpose of the building was not just to announce the goring power of the railway in the Dutch colonial outpost, but also to demonstrate to the locals just how capable their overlords could be. The design was a propaganda tool, a warning to those in the area that they were existing under the yoke of imperial order. The four buildings, surrounded at all times by a high fence, are intimidating and domineering. Down to the last brick, the building was intended to convey and important political message. That the A building looks so much like a church is no mistake, as religion was another important means of control. Elsewhere in the ground, the red-tiled roof recalls the similar designs in the Netherlands, while a ballroom was included to provide a place for the colonialists to enjoy themselves.

Some of the most interesting additions have, surprisingly, lasted the longest. Despite the rot and decay that has set in elsewhere, the building also boasts a set of stained glass windows that have endured to this day. Depicting various cities back in the Netherlands, these colored windows are arranged to catch the morning light and emit an ethereal glow to those who pass into the building. Added to the sheer volume of doors and the fact that Lawang Sewu rises up out of a relatively flat part of the city, the intent was surely to impress, coerce, and perhaps even threaten the locals into submission.

But the differences between the Lawang Sewu and the local buildings runs deeper than just the bricks. Entering through the main entrance has been likened to walking into a church erected in dedication to the advances of Dutch technology at the time. Not only are the stained glass windows immediately apparent, but they're utterly alien in the context of Indonesian building practices. They are just another tribute to the Dutch rulers, which is why they depict cities in the Netherlands where one might normally expect to see biblical stories. But factors such as this are not just empty boasts of better technology. The argument for the Dutch colonial rule was often that they were aiding the local communities they controlled by bringing advances such as the railway and stained glass to their doorstep. Regardless of how many Indonesians they killed, or how much of the local wealth they plundered, they operated under the guise that they were actually helping people in the area. One of the best representations of this is the railway itself. Just as the building is a tribute to the railway and the Dutch technologies that made it possible, it is at the very same time a tribute to the brutal colonial rule that was carried out in the country. If that is not enough to elicit negative emotions and paranormal activity in an area, then what is?

But the Dutch rule in Indonesia did not last. The outbreak of World War II brought fresh troubles to the Netherlands, and soon, the majority of the country's efforts were dedicated to issues at home rather than abroad. This left them wide open for other expansionist colonial powers in South East Asia to fill the power vacuum they had left behind. As the Dutch began to retreat from the area, it was not the local Indonesians who took back control of the country. It would turn out to be someone far worse.

The Japanese invaded the country in 1942. It was not long before they had taken over from the Dutch as the colonial masters, and as part of an already functioning war machine, their tactics were much more brutal. While the Dutch had ostensibly ruled in peace (violent colonial peace, to be sure), the Japanese took over the country by force and ruled by force. They snatched up the former Dutch seats of power and turned them to their own uses. Now, rather than an office for the Railway company, Lawang Sewu saw its history take a darker turn.

The basement of Lawang Sewu was originally designed as a prototype air conditioning system. A huge empty room, the basement would be filled with cool water and then the cool air would billow around the building. When the Japanese moved in, it was turned into a prison. All of the B building was repurposed as a detention center, a place where the Japanese army could store those who fought against them or that they found otherwise undesirable. To this day, the violence they used remains an essential part of the history of the building. They tortured, beat, and executed untold numbers of Indonesians, to the point where the building became closely associated with death and pain. If you were taken to Lawang Sewu, then it could only mean that you had pain to come in your very immediate future. Even if you were lucky enough to escape, it would likely mean that you had been brutalized and mutilated beyond all recognition.

The stories of the vicious rule of the Japanese army have entered into local folklore. One such story involves a group of prisoners who had been sent into the detention center. Space was getting crowded inside the giant cellar of the B Building, but that did not stop the army officers from beheading the prisoners and hurling their heads the length of the room. Eventually, the decapitated heads were piled up in the corners of the room as men were walked through the center. To this day, people have reported hundreds of specters of headless figures wandering the grounds in a blind stumble.

But the Dutch story in the country was not over. By 1945, the Japanese had failed in their war efforts. American forces had begun an assault on the islands that culminated in the atomic bombs dropped on Nagasaki and Hiroshima. This, again, provided the Indonesians with the chance to take over their own country, and this time, they were better prepared. As they had taken over the city, a small cadre of Dutch troops watched on. Planning an attack, they used their knowledge of the tunnels under the Lawang Sewu to sneak into the center of the city without being noticed. The tunnel systems were more complex than anyone had imagined. Without the locals realizing it, the Dutch linked their railway headquarters with many of the most important strategical points around the city. There was a slaughter. The battle lasted for five days, all across the city, with men dying on both sides. Eventually, however, the Indonesians emerged victorious. For the first time in a very long period, they finally had control of their country. With it, they now had control of Lawang Sewu.

The forces who wrested back control of the city were not only armed men. The Indonesian youth were key to the battle and helped turn the tide against the colonial forces. To honor them and the rest of the fallen, there is now a monument erected opposite the main building. While there is a plaque commemorating and memorializing their efforts, it is not read by many people. The current state of Lawang Sewu means that few people feel the need to stop by and read the words.

There is a constant belief that the building is haunted. It is haunted by the country's colonial past and by the ghosts of the men who died such violent deaths on the grounds. For such a well-known building, it should perhaps not be surprising that it has fallen into such a state of disrepair. The paranormal activity that is so closely associated with Lawang Sewu means that people do not wish to go inside. Not only is it a macabre reminder of the period of colonial rule, but the very real torture and death that took place there leads many to believe that it is a hotspot for paranormal mysteries.

The stories that emanate from inside the building now deter people from entering inside. Despite being one of the most famous local landmarks, it is well known that those who step foot inside the railway station can potentially incur the ire of the dead. Those who have been inside and spent any amount of time there have returned with mysterious stories. Like many other paranormal sites, the sounds of scratching, whispering, and footsteps echo through the corridors. From behind each of the thousand doors, it seems as though there is someone trying to get out. Those who have been there at night have reported witnessing the headless figures crawling around the grounds and along the hallways. For decades, these ghosts have been searching for their heads on the grounds and seem to be doomed to continue to do so for the rest of eternity. These days, one of the rites of passage for youngsters in the city is to sneak into the grounds and spend a few hours (or as long as possible) inside without becoming too scared. If you ever watched the building through the night, you might well see one or two audacious teenagers fleeing the building in terror as Lawang Sewu proves to be too much for them.

There is another enduring story of one particular ghost that seems to haunt the building and has appeared to many people. As well as the hordes of headless specters, it is said that one of the last people to die on the grounds was a Dutch woman. A member of the colonial forces who had hoped to reconquer the city, she witnessed firsthand the deaths of her fellow countrymen. As the Indonesian forces closed in, and she knew she was likely not long for the world, she took her own life. Before she died, she came to terms with the guilt and the reality of what the Dutch colonial masters had done to the city and the country. After hanging herself from one of the rafters, she now appears to visitors, emitting a low, throbbing groan and raising one solitary finger in their direction.

Stories such as this one are part of the reason as to why the building has fallen into such disrepair. For decades, there has been a lack of interest from the government in diverting funds to maintain the building's upkeep. Over time, this has led an already eerie and strange building to become even stranger. The moss growing up the walls, the cracked paint, and the plants emerging out of the walls give the feeling of the building itself dying around you. The stains on the walls and the missing tiles on the roof speak of a deep malaise, an illness built into the very walls. As it began to look more and more like a traditional haunted house, the tales about what happens in Lawang Sewu only proceeded to multiply.

But there have been recent attempts to banish the ghost stories from the public's mind. Starting around 2009, various government authorities have recognized that the building is iconic in design and important to the history of the city. They have hoped to renovate the building and to do away with the superstition that surrounds it. As a site with the potential to raise a lot of money from commercial, tourist, and real estate ventures, there is a growing need to prove to people that it is not simply a building filled with ghosts. An opening ceremony for one set of renovations seemed almost like an exorcism, with a concerted effort on the part of the developer to make it seem as though they were banishing the evil spirits from within. Since then, there has been much talk in the state-run press of how Lawang Sewu has been losing its "mystical air." While much of this work is commendable and will no doubt prolong the life of an important and fascinating building, there is a sense of hopelessness about the authorities' efforts. The more they do to dissuade people from believing in the haunted past of Lawang Sewu, the more they remind people of its terrifying history.

Banff Springs Hotel, Alberta

It should come as no surprise to see that there are many hotels in this list of the most haunted places in the world. Hotels often see a great many people pass through their doors in a short amount of time. While the majority of these people are simply hoping to spend a few nights in relative comfort, there are others who arrive with more nefarious purposes. There are those who have murder on their mind, those who are hoping to end their own lives, those who have criminal intentions, and those who simply wish to push the boundaries of what is acceptable to the very limit. With people from all walks of life arriving in a hotel at any one time, the spirits of those who die at the location can be varied, both in terms of their demographic and their intent. Often in hotels, you will discover a variety of different apparitions, each with their own unique story. This is certainly true of one of Canada's great old hotels, the Banff Springs Hotel in Alberta.

When it was being built in the 19th Century, the owners of the Banff Springs Hotel wanted to make use of the most luxurious designs possible. Nestled away in the Rocky Mountains, it was part of a Canada-wide effort to link the country up via railroads, with luxurious hotels scattered along the cross country routes. The surrounding vista certainly cuts a dramatic scene. As mountains rise up on either side of the valley, the hotel bubbles up over a sea of pine trees. Carved on top of a rocky outcrop, the hotel is an island in the middle of the wilderness. Its distinctive roofline is made all the more iconic by the lack of buildings anywhere nearby. Seen from a distance, it could not be more isolated. It sits against the backdrop of Mount Rundle, a site frequently hailed for its tough and rugged exposed ancient sea beds. It all adds up to a strange sight.

But this isolated nature of the hotel, while adding a scenic beauty, certainly adds to the fear factor when people check in. Thanks to its reputation as one of Canada's most haunted sites, few people who travel all the way out into the middle of nowhere are unaware of the building's paranormal history. Once they have reached the front doors of the hotel, there is little in the way of nearby help that is available to them.

The problem has been something the current owners of the hotel have tried to combat. The Public Relations Department of the Banff Springs Hotel have released official statements assuring guests that the building is, in fact, not haunted. Their insistence on the hotel's lack of ghosts has failed to ring true with the general public, however, and the location's paranormal reputation continues. There is a desire on the part of the media to delve deeper into the truth behind the hotel, and several years ago, one team began to investigate matters by interviewing (anonymously) various members of staff who had spent extended periods of time in the hotel and had heard stories from colleagues and guests, as well as seeing ghostly activity themselves.

The history of the Banff Springs Hotel encompasses almost 150 years. Construction started in 1888, intending to ape European designs from the Tudor period in England or the various chalets around Switzerland. It has changed somewhat since then, with the design intentions expanding and becoming grander and grander with each step. A key mistake was made during construction. What had been intended to be a hotel with an expansive view of the mountains was in fact built facing the wrong direction. With its back turned on the expansive view, the original layout featured a hundred rooms over five stories, which was expanded to 200 rooms in 1902. Over time, more and more additions were stuck to the side, the top, and the edge of the hotel. In 1906, for example, the owners planned to completely overhaul the design. This would involve replacing many of the original sections. Key to the plan was an eleven story central tower to dominate the roofline of the building. They hoped for reorientation of the hotel and to get their original view back. Finally finished in 1914, the tower alone cost over $2 million, a huge amount of money at the time, and a move that made the building the tallest in all of Canada. The hotel continued to be fine-tuned and tweaked, with expansions added over time, until a fire in 1926 destroyed much of the original structure.

For much of the hotel's life, the Canadian winter made it impossible to stay there during the colder months. This would mean that the guests would vanish when the temperature plummeted, while the building would survive with a skeleton staff, people who were employed simply to keep the snow on the outside of the building and ensure nothing went wrong. Forced to remain in one place for the entire season, these custodial members of the team would be left alone for months at a time. Out in the cold isolated sparseness, questions were often asked about their sanity. This changed in 1968, when modifications to the hotel made it possible to remain open during the winter. Since that time, the Banff Springs hotel has welcomed guests all year round. The question remains, however, of whether anyone was ever truly alone in what is considered to be one of the country's most haunted buildings.

It seems as though everyone was amazed by the success of the hotel. The constant expansions, despite the seeming isolation of the resort, were often planned furiously and carried out as quickly as possible, in order to fit as many guests into the luxury hotel as possible. But as with the original builder whose mistake meant the building was facing the wrong way, the efforts of one of the expansionist construction crews meant that there was in fact a secret room built into the hotel. At first, it was just an oversight. There was an error with the reading of the architectural blueprints, leading to the construction of a room without any doors and without any windows. In a rush to finish the job and not raise the ire of the building owners, the construction crew covered up their mistake and altered the blueprints accordingly. It was only the fire in 1926 that revealed the secret room to the owners of the Banff Springs. By that time, it was already written into the history of the building.

After the fire, the process of cleaning up the affected areas of the hotel was carried out in a similarly furious rush. Before the Banff Springs was altered to be a viable business proposition during the winter, any kind of downtime severely affected their opportunities to make a profit. A fire was a hindrance, but it could be cleared up and guests moved back into the rooms in no time. It was during part of this clean up, however, that the workers noticed a strange addition to the hotel, one placed where no one had previously thought to check. As revealed by the damage of the fire, there was an additional room that stood without any windows or doors. It was inaccessible, immune to light. It was just as the builders had left it when they had bricked it up to cover their mistake. But that most intriguing aspect of the secret room was its location.

For a long time, tales of the paranormal had been passed around the hotel. They were handed down from staff member to staff member, originally arriving from either the staff themselves or the guests who thought it right to report odd behavior to the front desk. Even several decades after the construction of the corridor containing the hidden room, there were still reports from people about mysterious happenings along that stretch of the hotel. In particular, some of the hotel's security guards had often reported a shadowy figure moving along the walkway, past the secret room. But when they had chased the figure down, they had found nothing. After this happened several times, more and more people began to report similar stories.

When trying to discern the identity of the figure, historians have come up against their own brick wall. Sealed off from the moment of its creation, the secret room was inaccessible to anyone else. Some people have suggested that it was the location for a secret society to perform various rituals, away from prying eyes. The guests would check into the hotel, one of them securing the room next door. When inside, they would pick apart the bricks and mortar in the wall and create an entrance into the hidden space. Once the group was inside, they could essentially do what they wanted. The shadowy figure, then, would appear during the times the group was in session and vanish when they were not there. The room might have acted as a gathering point for those with nefarious and illicit purposes, conducting sordid, satanic acts in a room no one else knew about.

But this begs the question, how did they come to know about the hidden room? This leads us into the next suggestion. The architect who designed the expansion to the hotel knew he had failed to carry out his job correctly. Already an ill, haunted man, he was troubled by many demons. The worry that his bosses might find out about the room plagued his mind and the paranoia that it might affect his career ate into his day-to-day life. It was a wasted room, a missed opportunity to squeeze in another paying guest. Frightened that the hotel owners might find out about the error, he was the one who had the room bricked up and who altered the architectural blueprints. But the mistake troubled him too much. Years later, he took his own life, the existence of the room enough to drive him to the edge. It is his ghost that wandered the hallways, trying to ward people off the discovery. Following the clean-up after the fire, the room was removed from the hotel. Coincidently, that particular ghost was never seen again.

Another of the more famous spirits that is said to haunt the hotel is that of a man named Samuel McCauley. Arriving in the 1930s, Sam McCauley heralded from Scotland and arrived at the Banff Springs with the intention of becoming a hotel porter. He was employed by the hotel and soon became an indispensable member of staff. He worked there for forty years in all, in various positions and with increasing seniority. By the time he died in the 1970s, he was as much a part of the hotel as the walls and the furniture. To many repeat guests, he was a recognizable face, a trusted member of staff whom they could depend upon to see whenever they arrived through the hotel doors. It should be no surprise to discover that death was not the end of Sam McCauley's time at the Banff Springs Hotel.

A familiar story coming from guests is the lights that often appear late at night just outside the rooms' windows. Always from rooms above the ground level, the guests on the second, third, fourth, and fifth floors sometimes arrive at the front desk, telling strange stories about the bright light they could see. Once stepping outside in the morning after the mysterious light appears, the guests can look up and discover that their rooms are on the face of the hotel that has no ledges and no place in which a person could reasonably place themselves. The lights are a mystery, but some have suggested that it is Sam, checking in on the guests to make sure that their stay is going well.

One couple in particular noted the same phenomena. They arrived at the hotel late after a long day's travel. Exhausted, they checked in well after the usual time and made their way to their room on one of the upper floors. They spent the night and arrived the next morning at the front desk asking about the identity of the man who had been so kind as to help the tired guests with the luggage as they made it to the top floor. He had been an older gentlemen, certainly well into his fifties. When the staff rotas (lists showing when each of a number of people has to do a particular job) were checked, there was not a single bellhop over the age of thirty working the night before. Similarly, when asked, none of the staff could remember seeing anyone help the couple with their bags. Perturbed, the man on the front desk tracked down one of the longer serving members of staff and passed along the description the couple had given about their late night helper. After listening to the description, they were astonished to discover that it was an exact fit for Sam McCauley. By this time, he had been dead for two years.

It is said that those who want to catch a glimpse of Sam McCauley for themselves need only travel to the top of the highest point of the hotel. The castle-like towers, added to the hotel over the years, contain nine floors and some of the more expensive rooms in the hotel. As the staff tell it, this is where Sam always used to be sure he would get the best tips. After four decades spent lugging bags up the tower and nine flights of stairs, even the spirit of Sam McCauley knows that this is his best chance for a handsome tip. If you'd like to visit the old bellhop, then this is the best place to track him down. The legends state that Sam knew the tower so well that he had stashed away four decades worth of earnings somewhere in this part of the hotel. Dying before he could spend his tips, still searching to add to his pile, he patrols the staircases in search of guests to help and inquisitive members of staff to ward off.

One of the most populated haunts is the part of the hotel known as the Rob Roy Lounge. Nominally a bar and an area designed for relaxation, it has nevertheless built up a reputation as being the primary destination for anyone who has an interest in the hotel's ghostly past. While the spirits in this section of the Banff Springs are more frequent, they are harder to document. Perhaps due to the crowded nature of the paranormal in the Roby Roy Lounge, many people have spotted different ghosts, but few specters have been sighted on repeat occasions. There are stories such as the bagpiper who is missing a head, the bride who perished when tripping down the hotel's staircase, and one of the longer serving bartenders who returns to the bar after his death to let certain patrons know when they have had more than enough to drink. These tales are rich in history but have been harder to confirm. Unlike Sam, their lack of regular sightings makes them difficult to add to the hotel's roster of the paranormal.

Other parts of the hotel have reported supernatural activity but not on the same scale as the lounge. One particular women's restroom is said to be haunted by the sound of a male voice, singing songs to anyone who walks in at around 3 o'clock in the morning. A similar phenomena occurs in the men's restroom nearby, though rather than a solitary singer, there is a chorus of voices who serenade anyone unlucky enough to be caught in the wrong place so early in the morning.

The hotel's MacKenzie room is home to one of the most unique ghosts said to exist in the Banff Springs. The room takes its name from the huge oil painting that is hung on the wall, with the room itself named after the man who is the portrait's subject. This is the same man whose spirit is said to have remained with the picture long after his death. Allegedly linked to the great fire in 1946 that destroyed much of the hotel and was mostly centered on the north wing, the portrait cuts an intimidating scene as it hangs over the room. People who have seen

54

MacKenzie's ghost report that the eyes are the source of the paranormal activity. Immediately captivating, they follow the viewer around the room like those in many great art works. But the difference in the Banff Springs is that MacKenzie's picture has a habit of coming alive. After moving around and settling on a target, the spirit itself comes out of the eyes of the portrait, bringing MacKenzie himself to life.

Like many of the entries on this list, the reputation of the Banff Springs hotel has become part of the building's enduring legends. As well as being one of the greatest old hotels in Canada, the Banff Springs has a reputation as being a hotspot of paranormal activity. This, in turn, attracts people of a certain disposition, people who actively hope to track down strange spirits. This feeds into the myths and the legends around the building, as the supernaturally inclined people begin to discover more and more about the history of the hotel. As well as the striking beauty of the surrounding mountains, the Banff Springs Hotel's reputation is well known. There is an apocryphal tale about a hockey team who stayed the night many years ago. Determined not to show any fear, the players steadfastly refused to tolerate the idea that there may be ghosts in the building. That is, all of them bar one solitary rookie, whose youth seemed to outrank his cynicism. The other players noticed this and decided to play a prank. As they prepared to go to sleep, one of the older players hid beneath the rookie's bed. Just as the youngster was about to lay down, the older player reached up and grabbed his ankle. The rookie was terrified. He knew the stories about the Banff Springs and hurled out of the door, screaming and shouting as he ran down the corridor to the front desk. As the rest of the players laughed, the staff didn't seem to find the joke quite so funny. While the hockey team left without further incident, those who have been in the building a long time know that there are just some things you don't joke about. In the case of the Banff Springs Hotel, there is always the possibility that a ghostly presence might be lurking around the next corner.

The Myrtles Plantation, St. Francisville, Louisiana

We have already seen just how much the past can influence the current supernatural activities surrounding a building. For the next entry in our list, we will again turn toward the United States, this time travelling to the South in order to learn more about a common fixture of 18th Century life in Louisiana, the plantation.

The history of the plantations in the South is very complicated. While many were large estate owners who had many slaves and worked them under often terrible conditions, others were more benign and simply shared the name without many of the moral complications. In the case of the home built by General Bradford in 1796 (first named Laurel Grove,) the building was a retirement prospect built by a disgraced general who had taken part in the so-called Whiskey Rebellion, an uprising against taxes levied by George Washington's government against certain alcoholic beverages in order to raise money for the still-young country.

Then under Spanish control, Bradford arrived in Louisiana and obtained a grant from the Spanish government to build a plantation on 650 acres of land. From here, he built up a business using slaves to plant, grow, and harvest the crops he then sold at a profit. Always an astute business man, he was known for his enterprising skills. Bradford was pardoned for his role in the Whiskey Rebellion and was then allowed to bring with him the family he had been forced to leave behind in Pennsylvania. He died in 1808. What he did not know at the time of construction his plantation, however, was that the site was not as empty or as hospitable as he might have thought.

There have long been rumors that Bradford constructed his home on the site of an ancient Native American burial ground. These sites, scattered across North America, have long been thought to hold mystic powers, with the idea being that they are finely tuned to the local paranormal forces. Often, the sites might be chosen for their inherent connection to the spiritual world, making them a good place for the various tribes to bury their dead. Centuries later, when the European settlers and their descendants began to build homes on the land, the damage and destruction they brought with them is said to have angered the spirits resting on the site. With the barriers between the real and the supernatural already incredibly thin at these sites, the construction of a huge house can be enough to attract an even greater paranormal force. It should come as no surprise, then, to learn that the house General Bradford built has a long and storied history of ghosts.

When it was built, the original home was much smaller. Always a mansion, it is a fine example of the antebellum plantation houses popular at the time. Built as what is known as a frame mansion, it does not rise high into the air. Instead, it is low and broad, sitting squat on the Louisiana ground, adorned with a clapboard exterior. The first six bays on the western facing side were part of the original build, while the rest were added during a major expansion carried out throughout the 19th Century, a process that nearly doubled the size of the building. One of the most distinctive features is an unusually long gallery, a room that is given support by a railing made of cast iron, constructed in an ornate grape-cluster design. The interior decoration, however, gave the building much of its reputation and was part of a redesign conducted by Bradford's descendants.

Despite the Myrtles being built on an Indian burial ground, it was a happy home for many of its first years, at least for those who lived in the main house. In order to function, the plantation required the use of slaves. African slaves were brought to the home, much like elsewhere in America, and put to work. Conditions were harsh, sometimes including physical beatings, forced labor, and the possibility of spending the rest of one's life working under the yoke of the plantation owner. Add to this the position of the building atop an Indian burial ground, and perhaps exacerbated by ancient mysticism and witchcraft carried out by slaves (including tales of voodoo,) there was certainly more than enough cause for the house to take on a more paranormal quality.

By 1817, the plantation was under the control of Clark Woodruff (a former law student of David Bradford), who married Bradford's daughter, Sara. They managed the plantation following David's death, also taking care of business for David's widowed wife, Elizabeth. Together, they had three children, and for them, life on the 650 acre estate was very pleasant indeed. However, it did not last. Over the course of 1823 and 1824, Sara and two of the children contracted yellow fever. The disease incredibly difficult to treat at the time and was usually deadly. All three died. Clark Woodruff and his one remaining daughter were left alone after Elizabeth also passed away a few years later.

But that is not the only version of events. Another version of the legend suggests that Sara was suspicious that her husband was involved in an illicit sexual affair with one of the slave girls from the plantation, a maid who worked in the house. One day, her suspicions grew too much. She followed the pair and watched as they made their way to the nursery where the children played, working up the courage to thrust open the door and see just what her husband and the slave girl were up to. Having spent a long time nervously pacing up and down the corridor, Sara finally threw open the door to find her husband and the girl caught in the act. She ran from the room.

The maid did not know what to do. As Clark chased after his wife, she was left alone not knowing what punishment might be fall her. She might be beaten, forced to work in the fields, sold away, or even something much, much worse. The girl tried to come up with a plan. Thanks to her close relationship with the children, she hoped that if the family fell sick, then she might be able to nurse them back to health and thus regain their trust. But the family wasn't sick. In order to instigate her plan, the girl took a number of oleander flowers and baked them into the family's dessert. The flowers were enough to poison the family, in particular Sara and two of her children. But they worked too well. Before the young girl could nurse the family back to health, they died. When it became clear what she had done, the slave girl was hanged the next day. There have been tales of a ghostly maid who moves from room to room with a candle, searching for the children to nurse back to health. Her shuffling footsteps are made all the more unique by the sounds of weeping she emits as she passes through the halls.

The series of deaths took a toll on the family. Unable to remain on the plantation, Clark moved himself and his daughter to the nearby town of Covington in Louisiana and left a caretaker in place at the plantation. While life was drastically altered for the rulers of the estate, life for the slaves and the workers was just as harsh as ever.

Finally, in 1834, the entire plantation was sold to a man named Ruffin Gray Stirling and his wife, Mary Cobb. For the new owners, the house seemed in dire need of a redesign. They were the ones who doubled the size of the main building. They also changed the name of the plantation from Laurel Grove to The Myrtles. They took it upon themselves to order a great deal of lavish furniture from Europe, a very expensive process that is a good indicator of the amount of money that was being produced by the plantation. Despite their extravagant lifestyle, the Stirlings encountered much of the same tragedy as their forebears in the home. After welcoming nine children into the world, they were devastated when five of them died at a very young age. Ruffin Gray Stirling himself passed away in 1854 and left the Myrtles to his wife, Mary.

One of the most famous stories concerning the Myrtles started when Mary, now alone and needing to tend to the plantation, decided to hire some help. She turned to a man named William Drew Winter, a lawyer and agent who she felt she could trust, in part because he was married to her daughter, Sarah Stirling. Like her parents, Sarah lived with her husband on the plantation. She and her husband started a family, but like her parents, they were also struck down by tragedy when one of their six children died of typhoid at just three years old. A particularly rough time arrived in 1868, when the family' financial plight grew so bad that they had to sell their land and home, only to buy it back in 1870. But the truly memorable incident would come in 1871.

We don't know the exact details of William Drew Winter's death, but we do know that he died ahead of his time. According to legend, he was shot on the porch of the plantation house by a man going by the name E. S. Webber. The two had seemingly fallen out, likely over money, when Webber pulled out a pistol and shot Winter. Stumbling, dying, Winter tried to climb back inside his house and call for help. His feet pounded up the steps to the porch, but he died before he reached the front door. This was how he was found, lying in a pool of his own blood. Perhaps the most famous ghost story from the Myrtles involves the sound of William Drew Winter's footsteps as he tries to clamber back into the house, followed by a deep thud as he hits the wood. According to some of the staff who have worked on the plantation, any attempt to clean the spot where he fell is impossible. The mop or the brush will simply avert itself from the part of the floor that is likely still seeped in Winter's blood.

After the murder, Sarah and her family stayed at the Myrtles for another eight years. She passed away in 1878, with her mother dying just two years later. Stephen, one of Sarah's sons, inherited the plantation, which was by this time heavily in debt and struggling to remain open. It passed through a number of hands shortly afterwards, with Stephen selling the estate to a man named Oran D. Brooks, who in turn sold it on. It passed through the ownership of several people before being purchased, in 1889, by a man named Harrison Milton Williams. After Williams passed away, the huge grounds of the Myrtles were divided up amongst his heirs. The house itself was sold separately, and in the 1950s, came under the ownership of Marjorie Munson. For the first time, the Myrtles was now owned by someone who seemed in tune with the paranormal history of the building. While many people had noticed strange occurrences and the site had a history of hauntings, Marjorie was the first person who began to actually document and look into the specters that appeared around the home.

After further changes in ownership, the plantation was eventually turned into a bed and breakfast hotel by a couple named James and Frances Kermeen Myers. The pair were aware of the history of the building when they bought it. They began to build on the work of Marjorie Munson in attempting to document everything that had happened on the grounds and why it might come back to haunt the current owners. They released their findings in the form of a book. Soon the fame of the Myrtles as one of American primary haunted houses began to grow. But, if we are to look deeper, what kind of paranormal activity can one expect to see in the Myrtles Plantation?

Thanks to the Myrtles' popularity as a tourist destination, we have many account of supernatural happenings that have come from people who have chased down the strange and the inexplicable. Whether these stories come from those who were skeptical and are now convinced or were firm believers who had their world views confirmed, it does not matter. Thanks to those slave owners who were a violent part of the plantation's past, as well as all of the children and adults who died on the property, there are said to be over a hundred ghosts scattered around the grounds. These days, however, many people focus their attentions on the main house and what it contains.

When digging around for more information regarding the past of the Myrtles, an old book was discovered that hinted toward an awareness of something supernatural happening on site. Written in 1882, the book provides a warning to anyone who is visiting the property. According to the author, the plantation owners were determined to always keep the lights burning around the grounds. It was only when all of the lights went out that something strange and often scary took place. After this was noticed, certain members of staff and slaves were ordered to ensure that a candle or a lamp was kept burning throughout the night, every night. It is a tradition that has endured to this day, where a light is always lit on the front porch of the Myrtles, lest the ghosts emerge from the dark.

While the lights are left on at all hours, they are by no means a guarantee of safety lasting through the night. As the sun drops over the antebellum mansion and its Louisiana surroundings, the shadows grow longer and longer. The sounds – scratches and crawling, the pitter patter of unseen footsteps – suddenly start to take on new meaning. What might have earlier been dismissed as another guest or a mouse might be attributed to something darker. Still, with the expensive European furnishings that were imported by the past owners, the Myrtles is a luxurious place to stay. But the lavish expense of the chairs, tables, mirrors, and clocks does little to ward off the dead. It does even less to ward off the worries of the guests as the antique, angled furniture begins to cast shadows and catch glimpses of the light, flickering and reflecting at the corner of your eye.

The long annals of the history of the Myrtles – and a source of much of the grief that befell the owners in later years – can be traced back to the American Civil War. Communities such as the one in Louisiana were a prime target for the Union as they attempted to quell the Confederate uprising. From elsewhere in the county, reports of violent deaths and massacres began to spread like wildfire. Rumors of butchery might have been greatly exaggerated, but they added to a tense atmosphere on a plantation that was still very much designed to make money. In order to run the plantation at its most profitable, the owners required slaves. The Confederacy's fight against the Union was chiefly concerned with the right to own slaves, so a loss in the Civil War might severely impact the plantation's ability to function. For the owners, this could be cataclysmic. For the slaves, it might have been a chance of escape. With this in mind, seven of the eight sons of the Stirlings (owners at the time) took up arms to join the Confederate army. Only one survived. It has been said that the specters of the Stirling soldiers have been seen around the grounds, preparing to defend their property against any Union attack. After their violent deaths, the Stirling sons have never found peace.

Taking place in the 1980s, a film crew tried to document an event known as the Myrtles Plantation Murder Mystery Weekend, during which a number of guests were invited. They would dress up in 19th Century clothing and go about their business as though it was a hundred years ago. Guests were even encouraged to try and talk about topics that might concern their 1871 counterparts, while they danced to the tune of a string quartet and enjoyed a feast that included a whole roast pig.

At the centerpiece of the re-enactment was a re-staging of the murder of William Drew Winter. Taking place on Saturday night, the murder would then be up to the guests to solve, just as they might in more conventional murder mystery weekends that had become popular during the 1980s. Such was the attention to detail put into the production, that the "murder" was intended to take place at the right time and place, down to the exact minute the real Winter had been murdered 114 years earlier. The death still came as a surprise to the guests, who were unaware of exactly what would happen. At the right moment, as they gathered near the front of the house, a voice – unseen – announced that it had arrived to visit "the lawyer." The actor who had been hired to play Winter stepped out onto the front porch to answer the call. A series of shots rang out. Everyone was surprised. The wounded William Drew Winter stumbled back into the home, blood pouring down his shirt. Searching around for his beloved wife, he could only crawl so far before he collapsed on the exact stop where his real counterpart had died years earlier. So far, everything was going just as the organizers had planned.

Then the lights went out. The entire home was plunged into darkness. Thinking that this was still a part of the production, the guests waited around to see what would happened next. However, this was not part of the act. The producers searched around desperately to restore power to the home. Eventually coming to the fuse box, they opened it to find that the internal working had been damaged beyond repair. It had broken at the exact moment – 114 years later to the second – when the man portraying William Drew Winter had fallen to the floor. The fuse box itself was inaccessible to anyone, as it had been locked. Fetching the key took a long time simply because no one knew where to look.

When they finally restored some power to the home, the lights turned back up. The now bemused guests rubbed their eyes as they discovered that all of the pictures and mirrors in the home had been shifted. They were still hanging, though everyone was tilted to the side, off-center. Some of them were now even hung upside down. Most people's gazes were eventually drawn to one portrait, a young woman whose picture had been hung above the piano. The figure in the portrait was now crying. Clear, watery fluids were visibly pouring out of the woman's eyes, while the piano meant that no one would have been able to reach up and alter it in anyway. The shaken guests decided to continue with the murder mystery weekend. William Drew Winter's murder was still there to be solved, regardless of whether spirits from another plane were trying to interfere or not.

But the story does not end there. As the owners of the home were helping the crew pack up and clean the home after the guests had left, they began to notice changes in the house. Whereas before, they could rely on the home to produce the ethereal sound of footsteps on the front porch every night, supposedly the ghostly steps of Winter's last, desperate attempt to find his wife, they were no longer there to be heard. To some people, it was almost as though the re-enactment of the murder had been enough to dispel and quieten a tormented spirit. To these people, the blowing of the fuse box and the jolting of the pictures were indicative of the spirit's attempt to leave our world. As Winter's ghost was able to finally find peace, it left in a dramatic and shocking fashion.

We do not have the space required to delve deeply into the background stories of the supposed legions of ghosts that are said to inhabit the Myrtles. As one of the buildings in this list that is actively welcoming visitors to stay the night and experience the specters for themselves, perhaps the best way of understanding the variety and scale of the haunting is to go and visit the site yourself. However, with such a long history of violent activity and so many links to death and spiritual mysticisms, it should really come as no surprise to see that the Myrtles plantation is one of the most haunted buildings in America, if not the world.

Okinawa, Japan

From a Louisiana plantation, we now travel to the other side of the world. As stretched out and open as the Myrtles plantation might have been, not all ghosts are thought to inhabit such a luxurious location. In Japan, the Okinawa Cave is said to be one of the most haunted spots in the world; not only a deep, dark journey down into one of the strangest places on the planet, but also a location surrounded by similarly haunted spots.

Okinawa, like many places on this list, has a torrid history. Found some 400 miles to the south of the Japanese mainland, it saw a huge amount of violence and bloodshed during World War II. As part of the American invasion in the closing months of the war, it was the ground on which the United States asserted control of the region and began to launch long range strikes into the rest of Japan. The battle for the island lasted 82 days, involving the deaths of 12,500 American and 95,000 Japanese military personnel. This does not even include the lives lost in the caves, when people crawled in and were later buried alive by American combat engineers. When adding together all of the civilian deaths, it could quite easily reach 150,000 Okinawa residents. This is enough to measure up against the combined death counts of the bombs dropped on Hiroshima and Nagasaki.

Not all of the civilian deaths came at the hands of the Americans, however. Fearing that they might be captured and tortured for information, and scared of dishonoring themselves, many thousands of soldiers from Japan committed suicide. One attack launched by the Americans on the Oroku Peninsula resulted in nearly 4,000 sailors committing suicide in the hidden tunnels of the navy base. On its own, this one incident could rank among the biggest mass suicides in recorded history. After so much recent death and suffering in Okinawa, it should come as no surprise to learn that so many people consider the region to be haunted.

Visitors to Okinawa typically focus on the history of the region. At the center of this is the Peace Memorial Museum, which features many artefacts from the battle. Here, visitors can examine the bullet-ridden helmets or search through a computer database of those who died. There are even written accounts of the tumultuous period from those who survived, their own handwriting preserved. One such account comes from a Japanese man who was just 14 at the time of the war. The boy was hiding when he saw a woman bring her two children to the area as she searched for a cave in which she could hide from the American soldiers. Not finding a suitable spot, the family cowered under a tree while the boy watched from a nearby cave. The caves were full, but if someone else left, then the family might be able to squeeze inside. Before this could happen, a shell crashed down from the sky. A fragment flew off and killed the mother instantly. Her baby was still suckling at her breast, the older one clinging to his mother's arm. And that was just how they stayed from three days. The account remembers how, venturing out from his hiding spot to relieve himself, the 14 year old found the children dead as well, the cold finishing what the shell had started.

But both sides in the fight were capable of great atrocities. The Japanese occupation of Korea, China, and other countries during the period was often carried out with tremendous levels of violence. In Okinawa, it was not uncommon for the Japanese army to evict civilians from the protective caves in order to take cover themselves. In some circumstances, those who would not leave peacefully were simply executed.

In another part of the museum, there is a room dedicated to the pictures of the young girls who died during the fighting. Inside a huge room, rows and rows of the teenage girls stare out from old photographs. These images are juxtaposed against the accounts written beneath, in which it is described how these girls eventually died; their jaws blown off, their bodies blown to smithereens, how they were napalmed while inside caves, or how some of the girls used hand grenades in order to commit suicide rather than endure the rape they had been told that the Americans would no doubt inflict upon them, a result of the Japanese propaganda machine.

The caves themselves played a key role in the battle, and this is partly why they have such a supernatural reputation today. As a hiding place, they were perfect for those who hoped to flee the onrushing American forces. But they also functioned as a fortress, providing the location for command centers for the Japanese army that were naturally well fortified. Buried deep inside the system of caves is one particular space, known as the Chibichiri Cave. It's a natural cavern and measures roughly a 100 feet deep. It was the hiding place for 140 Okinawa villagers who fled inside when the Americans attacked. They had already been informed by the Japanese army that capture would mean torture and execution at the hands of the evil Americans. So convincing was the propaganda that two young boys tried to guard the cave from attack themselves, armed only with spears they had made by bamboo. They were shot and killed.

The Americans peered into the entrance of the Chibichiri Cave, begging the civilians to come out and offer up their surrender. They even dropped leaflets inside (written in Japanese) informing the civilians that they would be treated well. They were not believed. As one little girl began to panic, she begged her mother to put her out of her misery. The mother obliged and killed her daughter. This set off a chain reaction, and soon, parents throughout the cave were killing their children before taking their own lives. Of the 140 civilians inside the cave, 83 were killed in this fashion. While many of the bodies were taken away by grieving families, to this day there are still piles of unidentified bones littering the floor of the Chibichiri Cave. With such a violent recent history, it should not be too surprising to learn that the caves now have a reputation for the paranormal.

Today, it is only the entrance to the caves that is made available to most tourists. Unlike many of the entries on this list, which are often hotels and tourist hotspots, the majority of the caves in Okinawa are off-limits to people. The dangers of potential earthquakes are often given for not allowing people inside, though some have suggested that it is the relatives of those who died that don't wish their ancestors' bones and teeth to be stared at by tourists or even pilfered as souvenirs. However, it is possible to get access to the rest of the caves. If a person writes in advance to the head of the volunteer group who oversees the caves, then it is possible to delve deeper inside the network of caverns. It is often only granted to those who wish to come and pay their respects to the dead, with the group being particularly wary of any Americans who might be arriving to celebrate the victory.

But what lies deep in the caves is not the only paranormal mystery in Okinawa. Though many of the worst atrocities and emotional turmoil occurred deep in the bowels of the region, this seems to have seeped up through the earth and spread across the surface. Visitors to other parts of the island can take in far more than they might ever have expected. All across Okinawa, there are hauntings that can make the skin crawl.

One of the first buildings tourists often encounter is a haunted apartment block. Travelling to the north of the Kadena Circle, leaving Highway 58, means coming face to face with a large, mostly abandoned apartment building. First opened with many of the lower floors used by a department chain, it was forced to close after failing to attract any customers. Before the abandoning the shop for good, there were stories of how children who would encounter other youngsters in the store, children who seemed to be in great pain and were often bandaged. The visitors might stop and play with these children, before running off to tell their parents. Soon, the adults caught on to what was happening and refused to allow their children to enter the store. Customer numbers plummeted.

These days, the abandoned lower floors are matched by the highest levels, where people refuse to live. Stories of hauntings linger throughout the top and the bottom of the building, and the paranormal activity is often attributed to the hospital that was built right next door after the end of the war. Since then, many children have claimed to have seen spirits inside the walls and when looking through the windows. It is said that any picture that is taken on the fourth floor will, when developed, be marked by the presence of previously unseen faces. For some people, these stories are often attributed to the dead who passed away in the hospital, their spirits getting caught amid the negative energy in Okinawa and getting stuck in the apartment building next door.

73

A similar set of stories revolve around a specific building on the Kadena Air Force Base. Known as Building 404, it is now the place where the Public Affairs office that the local government uses. Previously, however, it was the Army morgue used during the war. Those who have spent time in Building 404 have frequently reported strange activity, such as their possessions being moved around the room, constant shuffling and dragging noises, and even suggestions of dark shadows appearing on the wall. These stories extend to the rest of the Air Force base, with those who venture near the old morgue reporting the arrival of ghostly pilots as they begin to get ready for their missions, climbing into the cockpits of planes that were never set to return.

One reporter who had been working in the area told a story about a strange night he spent in Building 404. As he sat working in the photographic dark room, he remembered the sound of one of the outer doors being slowly opened. He thought nothing of it, thinking it was simply one of the offices workers finishing a shift. But as he turned back to his work, the reporter noticed a figure moving past the door once, then twice. Assuming the person wanted to be let in, he got up to open the door. Just as he reached the handle, the figure on the other side began to walk away. The reporter, his curiosity piqued, stepped out into the hallway and called after the figure. After receiving no response, he shouted louder and louder. At last, the shadowy figure spun around. According to the reporter, what he saw was not human. Instead, it was as though most of the man had fallen away, visibly exposing the skeleton beneath. Doling out a quick sneer, the strange apparition simply vanished into the air.

The story became something of a legend around Building 404. In response, one of the employees in the building gathered together a group who set out to bust the mystery. They set up cameras throughout the corridors. The group tried to stay up and monitor their equipment, but events soon took a merrier turn. Partying, they soon became distracted and eventually fell asleep.

At half past two in the morning, however, they were jolted awake. They all rose to hear the screeching of a chair being dragged across a floor. A freezing wind began to drift in to the room, bringing with it an unkind, negative atmosphere. What excitement there had been quickly turned to terror, and everyone left as quickly as they could. Returning later, they realized that they might still be able to develop the film in the cameras and discover just what had been happening that night. When they finally got their hands on the finished photographs, it seemed as though there was absolutely nothing out of the ordinary. The pictures were just as could be expected from a normal room. Apart from one. When examining a group photo closely, one of the employees noticed a strange man at the back of the crowd. No one knew him. None had even seen the man before. But he was stood there, with a weak smile traced on his face. To this day, no one has discovered the identity of the strange, smiling man.

Another of Okinawa's strangest stories relates to a restaurant that can be found near Yonabaru along Route 77. If you travel down the road, you will come across a restaurant that was never actually completed. To believe local legend, the story begins with an old woman who had three sons, all of whom were doctors. The first was able to construct a number of small businesses on the various plots of land that his mother owned across the island. They did not succeed, however, and before long the business went bankrupt and the son was in debt. To keep his companies afloat, the son borrowed money from dubious people. He drank heavily to try and deal with his woes. When the time came that he couldn't pay off the money he owed, the loan sharks moved in and forced his mother to sell all her land. Included in this was the restaurant in the midst of construction. A short time later, she died. Over the coming years, the restaurant remained unfinished, and no one dared to step inside. At a nearby fountain, the locals began to speak about an old woman who was spotted sitting by the water. When the restaurant was finally bought, the new owner was about to start renovating when things started going wrong. The carpenter quit after his lunch went rotten in just a few hours. He fled the scene with a terrible headache, and just as he was driving away, he turned around to see an old woman sitting on his back seat, waving. He checked again, and she had vanished. After he told his friends, no one would touch the restaurant. As the stories spread, it was simply left to languish. Now it's just another entry into the long list of haunted buildings scattered across Okinawa.

Today, the Banyan Tree golf course in Kadena is a good example of the modern population's desire to re-establish life on Okinawa. However, the golf course sits right next to a cave. Inside this particular cave, the Japanese army set up a field hospital during the fighting. As well as all of the amputations and deaths that happen in any conflict hospital, the site was witness to an even greater tragedy. Now known as Hospital Hill, it was the place where 17 nurses all used grenades to commit suicide just before they were captured. For anyone who ventures into the cavern right next to the golf course, the scorch marks from the blasts are still visible on the walls. These days, it is said that there is a strange wailing sound that emerges from the mouth of the cave and carries out across the golf course, sounding exactly like the last screams of the dead.

As with many of the entries in this list, however, it is a hotel that has been at the root of many ghost stories passed around Okinawa. Much like the restaurant mentioned above, this particular story focuses on a hotel that was never actually finished. Those who journey to what is known as the Haunted Hotel in Nakagusuku will encounter a half-finished shell of a building. On the inside, the sweeping staircases lead nowhere, and all of the luxuries that were installed at the time, now simply lie abandoned on the ground, left to the spirits within the walls. Thirty years after the end of World War II and the major fighting on the island, a businessman from Okinawa decided that he wanted to build a hotel. He picked out a specific plot of land in spite of warnings from the locals that this spot was sacred. The specific location of the hotel was only 50 yards from the ruins of Nakagusuku Castle had historically been persevered. Even during WW2, it had managed to stay mostly free of bloodshed, a rarity on the island. The warnings were ignored.

Construction began as the locals watched on. Much like the case with the restaurant, however, construction work seemed doomed from the start. During the building process, a number of workers fell to accidental deaths. Isolated incidents, these deaths occurred on site and concerned otherwise healthy, happy young men. Soon, it was enough to put off the rest of the crew entirely. In spite of the work that had already been done on the hotel, the other workers considered it to be a cursed project and refused to work. The businessman eventually went broke trying to finance the building of his dream hotel and could not finish it. No one bought it, and no one came to clean up the remains. Instead, it sits abandoned, just another tribute to the violent, haunting spirits that ebb and flow around Okinawa.

The recent history of Okinawa makes it obvious as to why it might be considered one of the most haunted places on earth. No matter what is built on the island, there is always an underlying suspicion and belief that it might somehow be affected by restless spirits. Those who died on the island might not necessarily be seeking revenge, but the violent manner of so many deaths in so short a space of time seems to have left a scar on the spirit of the island itself. Until that heals, it might be that Okinawa continues to keep a firm grip on its paranormal reputation.

But perhaps the strangest story from around the island is the next one. During the war, the Japanese soldiers had such an intense fear of being captured that it drove them to do terrible things. The propaganda machine that had been put in motion by the Japanese government fed into the idea that the soldiers from the United States were bloodthirsty barbarians, men who would horribly torture, rape, and kill without a moment's hesitation. This fear was so strong that every level of command in the army believed that it was better to kill oneself than run the risk of being caught. Suicide was the honorable option. One of the most popular methods of committing suicide was to jump from the cliffs that line the coast of Okinawa. As it became clearer and clearer that the war would not be won by the Japanese, more and more men began to line up along the clifftops.

Some of the bloodiest battles in the region were fought near Itoman. Thousands of men died in the fighting, and many more threw their lives away by jumping from the nearby cliffs. It is these cliffs that have built up a reputation in recent years, as those who venture up to the coast at night have reported seeing the spirits of these men as they abandon their lives. These so-called ghost jumpers can be seen running toward the edge of the land and throwing themselves into the rolling, crashing waves. For those who peek over the edge to search for any answers, the seas below are filled with thousands of ghostly faces, staring up in horror at what is happening above them. Today, many local residents of Okinawa refuse to travel up to the cliffs near Itoman. But, really, these ghostly figures who kill themselves night after night are simply another entry into the haunted history of one of the world's most paranormal islands.

Chaonei No. 81

The history of a building can have a huge impact on how people's beliefs and superstitions are shaped. Ghost stories and strange rumours often grow up around buildings in communities, but the more a building's history is secretive and hidden, the more people will be willing to believe in the existence of the paranormal hiding behind the front door. A fine example of this is Chaonei No. 81 in Beijing, China. The building is a fairly recent build, seemingly constructed in the style of the early 20th Century. But few people can remember it being built. Aesthetically different to the majority of Beijing's homes, it is no surprise to see that it has attracted attention. After mysteriously being abandoned for many years, it is even less of a surprise to learn that the locals are now convinced that the building is home to all manner of ghostly apparitions.

Any historical records we have of the building are sparse, to say the least. Trying to figure out who built the home is somewhat impossible these days, thanks in combination to lax record keeping and the level of bureaucracy surrounding Beijing at any one point in time. Due to the dramatic overhaul undertaken by the country when the communists took power in 1949, we may never know who built No. 81, but that hasn't stopped many legends being told by those who live nearby. Some have suggested that it was once owned by a man deeply embroiled in the Kuomintang (a political party that rivalled the communists) who fled the property when the revolution took hold. He supposedly left behind a wife, whose spirit is said to have remained long after her death. We have no way of confirming the story, however, and since the 1950s, the building has been owned and used by the Red Guards, various government organisations, and is now used by the Roman Catholic Church. After a number of occupants didn't stay for very long, stories about the property being haunted grew stronger and stronger. Due to its potential as a future embassy for the Vatican, repeated calls for demolition have been ignored. There's certainly something enchanting about the building, while being worrying in equal measure.

Chaonei No. 81 is in a fairly unassuming part of Beijing. Just a quarter of a kilometre away from a large intersection, the city has grown up around the old building. The Chaoyangmen gate is an ancient feature of the neighbourhood (and the place where the district took its name) but has since vanished. To all intents and purposes, the neighbourhood is a bit boring, a bit bland, and not very interesting. Apart from one building. These days – like the rest of the city – the area is densely populated and highly urbanised. It's a far cry from the traditional view of an isolated haunted house. Shops, businesses, and houses are all to be found just next door to No. 81, while a short row of trees does at least do something to hide away the building from the rest of the world.

These days, there's a concrete wall built up around the property. The building itself is accessible through a set of thin metal doors, though it's not usually encouraged for members of the public to enter inside. That hasn't stopped people, however. It's become quite proving ground for many young people in the city, who dare one another to venture in after dark. When these people sneak over the wall after the lights go out, they're met with three buildings. There's the main house, a second house which is even larger, and then a garage. The garden is not very welcoming, with no one having attended to it in years. These days, it's mostly just gravel and dirt, with the occasional plant attempting to take root and find somewhere to grow on the property. It's very rare that anything last too long, however.

The main house is the one that attracts the eye. Though not the biggest building on the plot, it's the one that occupies the thoughts of anyone who passes by. Walking east from the entrance, you'll come to the two and a half storey high building. It's finished in bricks, designed in a Flemish style. The roof rises to a peak in the centre and features a single brick chimney breaking up the skyline. From here, it's possible to see into the exposed basement which is directly below the ground floor. To the other side, there's a small pavilion that juts out from the building. The metal guttering that lines all of the roof top gargles and hisses in the rain and rattles in the wind.

Anyone walking up to the front door will have to ascend the large stone steps. A similarly stone balcony leers over the entrance, though it's taken the worst of the weathering with no one to clean it over the years. In some places, the stone work is damaged and the brick work ragged. It speaks of a building that's been abandoned and forgotten for a long time, making for an intimidating atmosphere and an unwelcoming feel to the façade of the main house.

There are not many people who know the property better than Xu Wen. As one of the groundkeepers at No. 81, he has spent a great deal of time caring for various parts of the property, though has been unable to prevent it from falling into disrepair. He has done what he can to tidy up parts and stop the spread of more deadly structural damage, but he is as equally confused about the history of the building as anyone else. He had labelled efforts to ascertain and exact history of the building as 'very difficult,' though he admits that the skeleton facts we have are likely correct. It's his opinion that the house started life as a language school in 1910, where they taught Mandarin to western missionaries. Later, they'd teach businessmen and diplomats the language, opening their doors to people who wanted to learn one of the most popular forms of Chinese.

Most of the stories we have of the building come from the current owners. Despite their inability to keep the building in the best possible condition, the Roman Catholic Church still use the property as their base of operations in Beijing. As such, they've taken on the role of history keepers in the region. In a country where Christianity is still something of an exotic and foreign concept, this adds another flavour to the already strange property. The church tells of how, during the Second World War, the building was used as a clinic. Augustine nuns from Belgium would treat people with a variety of wounds, meaning that it was fairly likely that people would have died nearby and often in great agony. When the Chinese Civil War was eventually won by the communist party in 1949, it was under the oversight of an Irish Catholic group who continued the work. To this day, Catholic influence in the area stems from the house. Despite the continuing presence of Holy men in the location, there has been no end of ghostly stories emanating from within. There have been little in the way of funds offered to the property's owners to help with upkeep over the years, and the government is reticent to offer huge amounts of assistance. In all, the appearance of the building, the presence of the Catholic Church, and the continued rumours of death and suffering within the walls have added to the paranormal reputation.

Many of the current stories about the property can be traced back to the 1970s. Before this, the turmoil of the Chinese government under Chairman Mao often meant that not only is the local culture difficult to penetrate for foreign media, but the huge storm of events at the time meant that there were often more pressing matters for the locals to focus on, rather than a potentially haunted home. But come the 1970s, more and more of the local legends were passed down and, soon, they were too loud to ignore. One local resident, Li Jongyie, can recall growing up nearby. The children would frequently play hide and seek in the property but would refuse to go in alone. They knew the stories well enough. Partially, these came from the Red Guards themselves. During the Cultural Revolution, the Red Guards were the ideological enforcers of the Chinese government and would often commit horrid deeds. Essentially a secret police force, they had carte blanche to carry out a string of torturous actions against anyone who didn't tow the party line. They occupied the building for just a few weeks – wresting control from the Catholics – before they exited just as quickly as they arrived. Even for their members, the building was too strange, daunting, and fearsome to remain within.

Compared to some of the other properties in this book, the list of ghosts thought to reside within the property is relatively low. While other locations might offer hundreds of spirits, No. 81 is home to just a few ghosts. Perhaps the most famous is the woman. She is thought to have been the wife of a member of the Kuomintang who once owned the home. We have mentioned him already, noting that he was called driven from the country by the war and was forced to leave behind his wife. She knew that it was a permanent arrangement. The couple had been very much in love, but should her husband ever return, she knew he would be caught and killed. Likewise, she had no way of journeying to meet him in Taiwan. She was despondent. One day, she was found hanging from one of the rafters. Stricken by grief, her spirit remained in No. 81. She lingers in the corridors, wanders the hallways, and appears before people searching for her long lost love. People have particularly reported having heard her calling out during thunderstorms. Her screaming voice is heard above the rain and the thunder, only to be matched by the screams of anyone silly enough to wander inside on such stormy nights.

The games of hide and seek played by the neighbourhood children have a darker side to them. For a long time, there have been rumours of people disappearing in the area. The mysterious house itself has been linked to these vanishing persons. One of these is a British priest, thought to have been among the people who built the property. The church members who currently operate the property have tried to discern his identity, but little is known about his character. We simply know that he vanished before he saw the house completed and was never seen again. To investigate his disappearance, a number of detectives were sent out. They arrived at the property and discovered that, not only had the man been planning to use it as a church, but that it was fitted with a number of secret tunnels that stretched out into the nearby neighbourhood. These were lost, filled in, or simply demolished over the years, or were simply forgotten about. The man himself was never found.

Another example of people vanishing near the property arose when three builders were dispatched to a nearby building to in order to carry out work in a basement. They set about their work for a short while but soon put it aside in order to get drunk. After a committed drinking session, they got back to work and decided that they needed to demolish one of the walls. It happened to be one that matched up with a basement wall in No. 81. They took a sledgehammer to the concrete and tried to break through to the other side. They were never seen again. For some people, this was the incident which prevented the government from demolishing the building in the 1990s. While the official line is that the Catholic interest in the building prevented its demolition, others have suggested that the government is wary of the strange tales that have emanated from within.

Like many stories in this book, finding the truth about Chaonei No. 81 is incredibly difficult. The manner of its ownership and the fact that it is not open to the public mean that it is not typically open for examination by paranormal investigators. We have, instead, to rely on the stories and accounts we get from the public. The list of paranormal phenomena associated with the property is long. One of the most consistent tales is that of the eerie, cold feeling which passes over pedestrians who stray too close. Whatever the weather, it's not uncommon for a passer-by to suddenly be struck by a feeling of utter dread as they walk by the property. Anyone who has ventured up to the front steps of the property in the warmer summer months has remarked just how much colder and more chilled the air around the entrance remains. Because of these legends, it has become impossible to sell or rent the property. The involvement of the Catholic Church is always a strange addition to the story, with many locals assuming there is something more to the Christian interest in the property – there are many more buildings in Beijing which would make a fine base of operations, without the ghostly reputation. But for those who visit the home now, one of the most recent adornments seeks to pacify anyone worried about the supernatural. Scratched into the wall next to the front gate is a warning for the daring and the scared. Written in chalk, it bluntly informs the world that there are no ghosts within. Whether the message is to be believed is another matter entirely.

The White House, Washington D.C.

The final entry in this book is something a little bit different. We have already seen how much a violent and bloody history can influence the supernatural in certain buildings. Typically, these are smaller, out-of-the-way locations where people are often scared to tread. But in this instance, the building remains one of the most famous and most important buildings in the world. Despite the tales that endure about the various ghosts that occupy the hallways of the White House in Washington D.C., it is still the seat of power in the United States of America and still home to the most powerful man in the world.

The house at 1600 Pennsylvania Avenue is undoubtedly the most famous in America. Over the years, it has been home to some of the most important men and women in history. Alongside the Presidents, First Ladies, Congressmen, and Senators who have walked the halls, however, it has also played home to huge numbers of regular people. These staff members might not be as famous, but they number in the thousands and are essential to the continued running of the White House. The lives (and sometimes the deaths) of these people all add up to what makes the building one of the most haunted in the world.

Those who have taken the tours of the White House (or those who remember any of its long and storied history), will know that the various rooms within the building all have special names, and often, special tales. In many instances, these singular rooms are home to more than just expensive furniture and anecdotes about foreign ambassadors. Take, for example, the Rose Garden. A familiar haunt of many Presidents, the Rose Garden lies just behind the Oval Office. It is used for many announcements and broadcasts, so it is likely that you may have caught a glimpse of it on television at some time. Designed and built by First Lady Dolley Madison during the first part of the 1800s, it is now nearly two hundred years old. It was, however, a century later when Ellen Wilson – then First Lady herself – asked for the workers in the building to dig up the Rose Garden. Just as the workers were about to break the ground and destroy the garden, they reported a strange vision appearing before them. A figure – bearing a striking resemblance to Dolley Madison – arrived and blocked them from accessing the gardens. They relented, as did Ellen Wilson, and the Rose Garden was allowed to remain. Since that time, the occasional burst of a rose-laden aroma has been noted around the White House. This, just like the saving of the Rose Garden, has been attributed to the ghost of Dolley Madison.

But not every ghost is human. The White House is huge – far larger than it appears to passers-by – and that includes a deep and complicated basement system. As well as the security measures and offices that are below ground, the dark, dank corridors are the seemingly perfect place to encounter a ghost. Rather than some kind of Presidential specter, however, the corridors in the basement are said to play home to the spirit of a long dead cat. Security in the building could not be tighter, and the thought of a stray animal sneaking into one of the most closely guarded buildings in the world seems unbelievable. But that does not stop the stories from staff members who claim to have met a cat below ground. According to the stories, the creature first appears as a tiny kitten, but that as soon as they move closer, the cat seems to grow and grow. The stories of this ghostly feline appear scattered throughout the annals of White House history, but they have often been connected to momentous, terrible events. Sightings in the 1920s and 1960s have been connected to the Wall Street Crash and the assassination of John F. Kennedy, respectively. In a time when security could not be tighter, it seems easy enough for a paranormal cat to ghost through the tightest of defenses.

The second floor of the White House is one of the busiest areas in terms of paranormal sightings. Both the halls and the bedrooms on this level have their own stories to tell, which is especially pressing as these are the residential areas belonging to the President and his family. Accordingly, many of these stories involve Presidents past and present, as well as their family members. The daughter of Lyndon B. Johnson, for example, recalled how she once encountered a ghostly boy named Willie while she was staying in one of the second floor bedrooms. It was only after she came across the boy's portrait in one of the halls that she realized that he was actually the son of Abraham Lincoln and had died many decades earlier.

The ghost of Lincoln himself is said to inhabit various rooms around the White House, including the second floor hallways. In total, Abraham Lincoln's ghost is the most commonly seen of all the spirits at the White House. It is not necessarily the ghost of the 16th President himself that appears before people, but as reported by some, his presence is felt in the rooms around the building. As one of the few Presidents who was assassinated while still in office, as well as the eventual winner of the American Civil War, his own life was filled with bloodshed. Despite his death occurring in 1865, it was not until the 1920s that his ghost was first reported in the Presidential home. Grace, wife of Calvin Coolidge, was perhaps the first person to witness Lincoln's ghost. According to her story, she came across the strange figure staring out through one of the windows in the Oval Office, out across the Potomac and toward the former battlefields of the Civil War that were so important to his tenure. For anyone who has spent any time in the White House, the image of Abraham Lincoln is immediately recognizable. Grace stopped and stared at what was appearing before her, convinced it was the man himself. She turned to try and find someone, but by the time she returned, the figure had disappeared. A similar story was told by Lady Bird Johnson, wife of Lyndon B. Johnson, who is said to have felt Lincoln's presence appearing to her while she watched a documentary show about his murder on a television. Before she could call out for help, the specter had vanished into the night.

It was during the Presidency of Franklin D. Roosevelt, however, that the most sightings of Abraham Lincoln were reported. These tumultuous years, lasting from 1933 to 1945 and throughout World War II, saw one of the greatest threats to the American nation since the days of the Civil War when Lincoln himself had been in charge. Again, it was the First Lady at the time, Eleanor Roosevelt, who first noticed the former President's presence in the building. She made regular use of Lincoln's former bedroom, turning it into something of a study for her work. While she spent late nights on a variety of different projects, she told stories about how she would feel Lincoln's presence creeping into the room. Always unseen, it was as though he were watching over her. Sightings were not limited to Americans. Queen Wilhelmina was visiting from the Netherlands and told the story about her stay in the bedrooms on the second floor. During the night, she heard a knock on the door. She answered, only to be met by the ghost of Lincoln himself, immediately recognizable thanks to his iconic black hat. As she fainted, the ghost vanished in front of her. Another visitor to the house, Winston Churchill, stayed at the

White House in his capacity as the Prime Minister of Great Britain. Visiting on a number of occasions during World War II, he emerged one night from a bath entirely naked apart from his customary cigar. As he stepped into the room, assuming himself to be alone, he was met with the ghostly specter of Abraham Lincoln, seated beside the fireplace. Churchill told the story with his renowned anecdotal skills, but friends could tell the incident shook him.

As ever in the White House, it was not only the First Family and foreign dignitaries that witnessed the extent of the building's haunted nature. A young seamstress named Lillian Rogers Parks was another witness to the ghost of Abraham Lincoln. She was working in the building and became curious about the constant sound of someone pacing back and forth along the upper levels of a room in the White House. Thinking no one should be up there, she set off to investigate. Once she reached the door to the room from whence the sound emanated, she held her palm over the handle. Opening the door and stepping in, she found nothing. The room was empty, bar the large portrait of Lincoln hung on the wall. When she talked about the incident with other members of staff, she was told that it was just "Old Abe" pacing back and forth in the room. It was a common enough thing to hear, especially during times of crisis. When things become particularly heated inside the White House, the occupants can expect to hear the footsteps of the former President as he moves back and forth through the building, mulling over the problems faced by his country.

Lincoln is not the only President whose ghost is said to haunt the White House. Andrew Jackson and Harry Truman have both been spotted on a number of occasions, while the ghosts of people such as Abigail Adams and David Burns (a major landowner in early Washington) show that it is not only the former heads of state who have remained behind. In a building with such a rich history as the White House, it should come as no surprise to see that there are many stories and legends that take the site as a starting point. Like the Tower of London many years ago, its importance seems like a shining beacon for the paranormal, with many emotions and energies lasting long after death. But unlike many of the other entries in this book, it is not a site that we will be properly allowed to investigate any time soon. Due to its importance to not only domestic, but also global politics, the days when we might conduct a thorough paranormal investigation into the White House might still be many centuries away. Until then, we will have to rely on the legends and tales to teach us about the building's haunted past.

Conclusion

Haunted house exist all over the world. Wherever people have died, the living will reveal stories about how they have encountered the dead in strange and often terrifying circumstances. Some sites, however, hold a certain attraction and appeal to the paranormal, it seems. Those places that are infected with negative energy, with great passions, and with tumultuous emotions often find themselves most prone to welcoming back the spirits of the deceased. As such, certain buildings – like the ones in this book – are often far more likely to hide away secrets between the bricks and the mortar.

There is little left to say about the world beyond our own. For those who are interested, there is a further reading list at the bottom of this page that can act as a jumping off point for further reading about the paranormal. For others, it is hoped that this book can act as a starting point for your own investigations in the supernatural. Once you have read through these accounts, if you still find yourself wanting more, you may need to take the next step and travel to these places in the flesh. Once there, you might find yourself at the center of a ghost story of your very own.

Further Reading

Brower, K. (2016). *Residence*. [S.l.]: Harpercollins.

Hall, W. (n.d.). *The world's most haunted house*.

Jones, R. and Mason, J. (2005). *Haunted houses of Britain and Ireland*. New York: Barnes & Noble Books.

Kermeen, F. (2005). *The Myrtles Plantation*. New York: Warner Books.

Lecouteux, C. (2012). *The secret history of poltergeists and haunted houses*. Rochester, Vt.: Inner Traditions.

May, A. (2006). *Haunted houses of California*. San Carlos, CA: Wide World Pub./Tetra.

Underwood, P. (1992). *The A-Z of British ghosts*. London: Chancellor Press.

Photo Credits

Tower of London Night 1, October 5, 2011, sksamuel

RMS Queen Mary in Long Beach, CA, June 2005, Sfoskett

Babenhausen Barracks, Nov 2008, ades_one

Ram Inn, Potters Pond, Wotton under Edge, 22 April 2008, Brian Robert Marshall

COLLECTIE TROPENMUSEUM Het hoofdkantoor van de Nederlandsch-Indische Spoorweg Maatschappij (NIS) in Semarang TMnr, KITbot

Banff Springs Hotel, October 1929, Banff Library and Archives Canada: PA-058085

A front view of The Myrtles Plantation, 7 April 2013, Cking81

The cave of Okinawa military hospital (dept. of surgery, 2nd div. in Itosu), 16 December 2005, A-gota

White House at night, 11 July 2010, SreeBot

About the author

Conrad Bauer is passionate about everything paranormal, unexplained, mysterious, and terrifying. It comes from his childhood and the famous stories his grandfather used to tell the family during summer vacation camping trips. He vividly remembers his grandfather sitting around the fire with new stories to tell everyone who would gather around and listen. His favorites were about the paranormal, including ghost stories, haunted houses, strange places, and paranormal occurrences.

Bauer is an adventurous traveller who has gone to many places in search of the unexplained and paranormal. He has been researching the paranormal and what scares people for more than four decades. He also loves to dig into period of history that are still full of mysteries, being an avid reader of the mystic secret societies that have mark history and remain fascinating and legendary throughout the times. He has accumulated a solid expertise and knowledge that he now shares through his books with his readers and followers.

Conrad, now retired, lives in the countryside in Ireland with his wife and two dogs.

More Books from Conrad Bauer

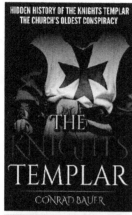

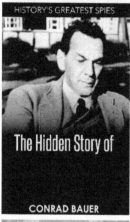
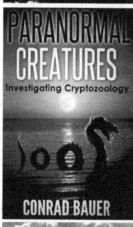

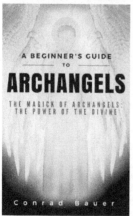